understanding
media economics

understanding
media economics

gillian doyle

SAGE Publications
London • Thousand Oaks • New Delhi

SAGE Publications Ltd
6 Bonhill Street
London EC2A 4PU

SAGE Publications Inc
2455 Teller Road
Thousand Oaks, California 91320

SAGE Publications India Pvt Ltd
32, M-Block Market
Greater Kailash – I
New Delhi 110 048

British Library Cataloguing in Publication Data

A catalogue record for this book is
available from the British Library

ISBN 0 7619 6874 1
ISBN 0 7619 6875 X (pbk)

Library of Congress Control Number available

Typeset by Keystroke, Jacaranda Lodge, Wolverhampton
Printed in Great Britain by The Cromwell Press Ltd,
Trowbridge, Wiltshire

CONTENTS

one

INTRODUCTION TO MEDIA ECONOMICS

The study of media and communications has traditionally been dominated by non-economic disciplines. Analysis of media content, for example, can provide a means of understanding the societies we live in and our value systems. But economics is also a valuable subject area for media scholars. Most of the decisions taken by those who run media organizations are, to a greater or lesser extent, influenced by resource and financial issues. So economics, as a discipline, is highly relevant to understanding how media firms and industries operate.

This book provides an introduction to some of the main economic concepts and issues affecting the media. It is designed for readers who are not specialists in economics but who want to acquire the tools needed to unravel some of the more interesting economic features and pressing industrial questions surrounding media firms and markets. No prior knowledge of economics is assumed.

The first two chapters explain a number of broad and fundamental concepts relevant to the study of economics as it affects the media. This opening chapter introduces you to firms and markets and it examines the distinctive economic characteristics of media. Chapter 2 focuses on the relationship between these special characteristics and the corporate strategies that are commonly deployed by media firms.

These initial chapters are followed by six others, each of which concentrates on a particular sector of media activity, e.g. television broadcasting, print media publishing or 'new' media. Sector-specific chapters are not intended to offer stand-alone accounts of the economics of each media activity. Instead, they provide a framework within which two or three of the main economic concepts or questions that are commonly associated with or best exemplified by that industry sector may be examined more closely. So, the structure of the book enables a series of economic themes and questions relevant to the media to be gradually and progressively opened up and explored. The final chapter examines what role media economics can play in informing public policy questions.

After studying this opening chapter, you should be able to:

- Identify the kinds of questions that media economics seeks to address
- Explain what a firm is, and its motivations
- Describe the different types of competitive market structures that exist
- Understand what is special about the economics of the media
- Identify and explain some of the key economic characteristics of the media

WHAT IS MEDIA ECONOMICS ABOUT?

Media economics combines the study of economics with the study of media. It is concerned with the changing economic forces that direct and constrain the choices of managers, practitioners and other decision-makers across the media. The economic concepts and issues introduced in the course of this book provide a basis for developing your understanding of the way in which media businesses operate and are managed.

Some attempts have been made to formalize a definition of media economics. Economics has been described as 'the study of how people make choices to cope with scarcity' (Parkin et al., 1997: 8). Scarcity is a familiar concept for most, and we are all economists to the extent that we have to decide how to make the best of our limited incomes or resources. According to Robert Picard, media economics 'is concerned with how media operators meet the informational and entertainment wants and needs of audiences, advertisers and society with available resources' (1989: 7). Likewise, Albarran's definition of media economics focuses on 'how media industries use scarce resources to produce content . . . to satisfy various wants and needs' (1996: 5). For Alexander et al., media economics refers to 'the business operations and financial activities of firms producing and selling output into the various media industries' (1998: 2).

Media economics, then, is concerned with a range of issues including international trade, business strategy, pricing policies, competition and industrial concentration as they affect media firms and industries. These themes are explored below, as each of the main sub-sectors of the media is examined in turn. The predominant focus throughout the book is 'microeconomic' (i.e. to do with specific individual markets or firms), but some of the questions addressed also have a macroeconomic dimension.

MACROECONOMICS AND MICROECONOMICS

The distinction between macro and microeconomics is about whether that which is being studied involves large groups and broad economic aggregates or small well-defined groups and individual firms and sectors. Macroeconomics is concerned with very broad economic aggregates and averages, such as total output, total employment, national income, the general price level, and the rate of growth of the economy as a whole. These sorts of aggregates are arrived at by summing up the activities carried out in all individual markets and by summarizing the collective behaviour of all individuals.

One of the most commonly used measures of a nation's overall level of economic activity is its Gross Domestic Product (GDP). A country's GDP represents the sum of the value of all goods and services produced within the economy over a particular period, usually a year. Media goods and services represent a small but growing proportion of total economic activity in developed countries and, in the United Kingdom (UK) for example, they account for some 3–5 per cent of GDP.

In the UK, the long-term trend in GDP since the Second World War has generally been upwards and this, in turn, has facilitated a substantial increase in living standards. Within this overall growth trend, a second feature of movements in GDP has been short-term fluctuations around the trend. Rather than growing at a steady and consistent pace, economies tend to move in a series of up and down 'business cycles' which are characterized by four phases: trough, recovery, peak and recession (Lipsey and Chrystal, 1995: 500–5).

The overall performance of the economy has important implications for the business performance and prospects of firms in all sectors, including media. Indeed, the fortunes of most media firms are highly sensitive to the ups and downs of the economy as a whole. Many media firms rely on advertising as a primary source of income. Analysis of long-term trends in advertising shows that there is a strong association between the performance of the economy as a whole and levels of advertising activity. Revenues for media firms from direct expenditure by consumers are also clearly dependent on broader economic aggregates such as levels of disposable income and consumer confidence.

In theory, public policies on the economy (monetary, fiscal, etc.), and policies to promote or restrain growth or social welfare may have an effect on the economic environment in which media firms and industries operate (Alexander et al., 1998: 9). For example, government control over the supply of money and over interest rates provides a means of influencing levels of investment and economic activity in general. However, it may be argued that the power of state authorities to exert such influence is waning. 'Globalization' means that it is increasingly difficult for open economies to predicate monetary and other economic policies on domestic considerations alone.

Whereas macroeconomics is about forces that affect the economy as a whole, microeconomics is concerned with the analysis of individual markets, products and firms. An economy is 'a mechanism that determines what is produced, how, when and where it is produced, and for whom it is produced' (Parkin et al., 1997: 21). These decisions are taken by three types of economic actors – consumers, firms and governments – and are co-ordinated in what are called 'markets'. Economics relies on certain assumptions about how these actors make their choices.

Each consumer, for example, is seen as having unlimited wants and limited resources. It is assumed that all consumers seek to maximize their total 'utility' or satisfaction. 'Marginal' utility represents the change in satisfaction resulting from consuming a little more or a little less of a given product. The law of diminishing marginal utility suggests that the more of a given product that an individual consumes, the less satisfaction he or she will derive from successive units of the product. The example used by Lipsey and Chrystal to illustrate this principle shows that, everything else being equal, the more films a consumer attends each month, the more satisfaction he or she gets. However, the marginal utility of each additional film per month is less than that of the previous one – i.e. marginal utility declines as quantity consumed rises (1995: 128–9).

THE FIRM IN ECONOMIC THEORY

In economics, production is defined as the conversion of resources – labour, land and capital – into goods and services. 'Firms' are establishments where production is carried out and industries consist of a number of firms producing a commodity for the same market. The concept of a media firm spans a variety of different types of business organization, from the online 'fanzine' publisher to the vast television corporation and from single proprietorship to major transnational Stock Exchange listed companies. What all media firms have in common is that they are involved somehow in producing, packaging or distributing media content.

All media firms are *not*, however, commercial organizations. Most countries have a state-owned broadcasting entity which takes the form of a public corporation and which is dedicated to 'public service' television and radio broadcasting. Many public service broadcasters (PSBs) rely on public funding (e.g. grants) but some depend, in part or in whole, on revenues derived from commercial activities such as sale of airtime to advertisers. Even when they compete for revenues from commercial sources, PSBs are usually distinguished from commercial firms by the fact that their primary goal is to provide a universally available public broadcasting service rather than to make a profit.

By contrast, it is assumed that a commercial firm's every decision is taken in order to maximize its profits. The assumption that all firms seek to maximize profits is central to the theory of the firm. It allows economists to predict the behaviour of firms by studying the effect that each of the choices available to it would have on its profits.

However, there are two commonly cited criticisms of the traditional theory of the firm and both are relevant to media. The first suggests that it is too crude and simplistic to assume that businesses are motivated purely by pursuit of profits. The case for profit maximization on the part of business owners is thought to be 'self-evident' but, in fact, some are undoubtedly motivated by alternative goals. These range from straight-forward philanthropy to the desire for specific benefits associated with owning certain types of businesses. An alternative motivation – especially in the case of media firms – might well be the pursuit of public and political influence.

A second criticism is that the theory assumes that all firms will behave in the same way, irrespective of their size and organizational structure. In reality, a firm's institutional structure may have an important bearing on its priorities. Rupert Murdoch's involvement in the running of News Corporation shows how some media firms are closely managed by their owners. But the dominant form of industrial organization these days is the public limited company (or plc) under which, more typically, the day-to-day running of the firm is carried out not by the owners (or shareholders) but by managers.

When ownership and control of an organization are separate, its managers may decide to pursue goals other than maximizing profits and returns to shareholders. This conflict of interest is referred to as a type of 'principal–agent' problem. The managers appointed to run a media firm (agents) may not always act in the manner desired by shareholders (principals) but might, instead, have their own agendas to pursue. When the agent's goal is allowed to predominate then pursuit of profits may be superseded by, for example, a desire to maximize sales revenue or the firm's growth.

There are good grounds for questioning how well the broad assumptions of conventional economic theory apply in practice to the behaviour of media organizations. Nonetheless, to the extent that media firms and consumers make their decisions in a 'rational' manner and in pursuit of what are assumed to be their own individual goals (of, respectively, profit and utility maximization), there will be a role for government to play in creating a regulatory environment within which these individual goals are not achieved at the expense of societal welfare (Alexander et al., 1998: 14). The issue of supplying violent media content provides an example of an economic activity that realizes the goals of one set of economic actors (i.e. it contributes to the success and profitability of film and television programme-makers) but, arguably, may detract from overall well-being of society (ibid.).

A firm's profits are the difference between its revenues and costs. Costs in economic theory refer to all 'opportunity costs' – i.e. 'the cost of using something in a particular use is the benefit forgone by (or opportunity cost of) not using it in its best alternative use' (Lipsey and Chrystal, 1995: 185). So, as well as assigning costs to purchased or hired inputs, an 'imputed' cost must also be calculated for and assigned to any factors of production owned by the firm, especially the firm's own capital.

The concept of opportunity cost is important in economics. Our resources can be used in many different ways to produce different outcomes but, essentially, they are finite. All of the land, labour and capital available to us will be relatively more efficient in some activities rather than others. Opportunity cost is inevitable and requires firms to make trade-offs. The most productive outcome will be achieved when every worker, piece of land and item of capital equipment is allocated to the task that suits it best (i.e. the one that results in the most productive outcome).

For example, if we want more educational CD-Roms and fewer computer games, we might switch some of the creative, marketing and administrative personnel, the computers and production equipment involved in producing computer games into CD-Rom publishing instead. However, because game inventors will be less good at creating CD-Roms than original educational CD-Rom publishing personnel, the quantity of CD-Roms produced will increase by a relatively small amount while the quantity of computer games produced falls considerably. Similarly, CD-Rom creators can be reassigned to the task of producing interactive computer games but, because they are not as good at this activity as the people who currently make computer games, there will be an opportunity cost in terms of lost output. The opportunity cost of switching resources from computer games to CD-Rom production (or from CD-Roms to games) can be calculated as the number of games that must be given up in order to produce more CD-Roms (or vice versa).

In order to maximize profits, firms need to decide which overall rate of output would be most profitable (e.g. whether to produce 100,000 or 200,000 copies of a magazine). To do so, they need to know exactly what costs and revenues might be associated with different levels of output. The so-called 'production function' describes the relationship between input costs and different levels of output. Changes in relative factor prices (of labour, capital equipment, etc.) will result in a replacement of factors that have become relatively more expensive by cheaper ones. For example, the introduction of new print and desk-top publishing technologies in the magazine publishing industry in the 1980s and 1990s reduced capital equipment costs and allowed a reduction in labour inputs.

'Marginal product' is the change in total product (or the total amount produced by the firm) that results from adding a little bit more or a little less of a variable input to a fixed input. The 'law of diminishing returns' suggests that if extra quantities of a variable factor (e.g. freelance technicians) are applied to a given quantity of a fixed factor (e.g. plant and equipment), the marginal and average product of the variable factor will eventually decrease. Picard offers the example of a television news director who is deciding how many news crews (whose labour represents the 'input') are needed to produce a newscast (the 'output'). The size of the marginal product increases at first, demonstrating increasing returns to scale, and then it begins to decline. According to Picard's example, the onset of diminishing returns occurs because, as more production crews are added and the use of production equipment has to be shared, the efficiency and productivity of each crew begins to reduce (1989: 53–4).

But contrary to what is implied by the law of diminishing returns, many media firms tend to enjoy *increasing* rather than diminishing marginal returns as their output (or, rather, consumption of it) increases. The explanation for increasing returns to scale in the media industry lies in the nature of the product and how it is consumed. The value of media content lies not in the paper that it is printed on or the ink or videotape that conveys its text or images but in the meanings, messages or stories that it has to offer – its intellectual property. This is an intangible and costs virtually no more to reproduce in large than in small quantities. The cost of producing a television programme or a film is not affected by the number of people who watch it. So, for media firms, the relationship between input costs and different levels of output tends to be skewed by the availability of increasing returns to scale.

COMPETITIVE MARKET STRUCTURES

As discussed above, the production function describes how costs vary at different levels of output. Firms that wish to maximize profits are not only concerned with costs but also need to know what revenues are associated with different levels of output. To a large extent this depends on what sort of 'competitive market structure' a firm finds itself operating in.

Economic theory offers us a model for analysing the different sorts of structures a market can have and the degree of competition between firms in that market. The competitive market structures within which media operate will have an important bearing on how efficiently media firms organize their resources and business affairs. The main theoretical market structures are perfect and imperfect competition (i.e. monopolistic competition and oligopoly) and monopoly. The distinction between these structures is largely dictated by the number of rival producers or sellers in a given market. This provides a significant indication of the 'market power' that individual firms possess and their ability to control and influence the economic operations in that market (e.g. to set prices). The less market power individual firms have, the more competitive the market structure they are operating in.

The structure of a market depends not only on the number of rival sellers that exist but on a variety of other factors, including differences in their product, the number of buyers that are present, and barriers to the entry of new competitors. Perfect competition and monopoly are at opposite extremes. In perfect competition, markets are highly competitive and open and each firm has zero market power. In monopoly, a single firm has absolute control over the market. Most firms tend to operate in some intermediate market structure rather than at the extremes.

Perfect competition exists when there are many sellers of a good or service that is homogeneous (i.e. exactly the same or not differentiated) and no firm(s) dominate(s) the market. In such a situation economic forces operate freely. Each firm is assumed to be a price-taker and the industry is characterized by freedom of entry and exit. So, under perfect competition, no barriers to entry exist – there are no obstacles (e.g. lack of available spectrum, or high initial capital costs) to prevent new rivals from entering the market if they wish. Monopoly, at the other extreme, involves just one seller, no competition whatsoever and (usually) high entry barriers.

It is very rare to find an example of perfect competition in the real world. Most industries, including the media, sell 'differentiated' products, i.e. products that are similar enough to constitute a single group (such as books) but are sufficiently different for consumers to distinguish one from another. In other words, they may be close substitutes but are not exact substitutes as would be the case in perfect competition. Monopolistic competition exists when there are a number of sellers of similar goods or services, but the products are differentiated and each product is available only from the firm that produces it. Firms thus have some control over their prices.

If there are only a few sellers in a market but some competition exists for their products, either homogeneous or differentiated, the market structure is described as an oligopoly. How few is 'a few'? The most usual method of measuring the degree of oligopoly in a market is by applying a 'concentration ratio'. These measures show the proportion of, say, output or employment or revenue accounted for by the top four or five firms in the sector. In the media sector, concentration levels can be calculated on the basis of audience shares (as defined by ratings or readership figures). According to Lipsey and Chrystal, in an oligopoly 'each firm has enough market power to prevent it from being a price-taker, but each firm is subject to enough inter-firm rivalry to prevent it from considering the market demand curve as its own' (1995: 262). So, in an oligopoly firms have a greater degree of control over the market than in a monopolistic competition.

Oligopoly is the most common type of market structure that media firms operate in. The next chapter addresses the question of why it is that so many sectors of the media are dominated by a few large firms. In many cases, the answer is to be found in falling costs due to the economies of large-scale production. Economies of scale are prevalent in the media because the industry is characterized by high initial production costs and low marginal reproduction and distribution costs. Economies of scope – economies achieved through multi-product production – are also commonly characteristic of media enterprises. So there are major advantages in large size for firms that operate in the media industry.

The theory of imperfect competition says that cost advantages associated with size will dictate that an industry should be an oligopoly unless some form of market intervention or Government regulation prevents the firms from growing to their most efficient size. If no such intervention takes place, existing firms in the industry may create barriers to entry where natural ones do not exist so that the industry will be dominated by a handful of large firms only because they are successful in preventing the entry of new firms. But substantial economies of scale in any industry will, in themselves, act as a natural barrier to entry in that any new firms will usually be smaller than established firms and so they will be at a cost disadvantage.

MARKET STRUCTURE AND BEHAVIOUR

The expectation that the behaviour or conduct of firms may be determined by the market structures within which they operate is formalized in what is called the Structure–Conduct–Performance (SCP) paradigm. The SCP paradigm suggests that market structure (the number of firms, barriers to entry, etc.) will determine how the firms in an industry behave (e.g. their policies on pricing and advertising) and this conduct will, in turn, determine the performance of the industry in question – i.e. its productive efficiency (Moschandreas, 1994: 11). This model implies that the fewer firms in a market, the greater the likelihood of collusion, anti-competitive strategies and other inefficiencies.

More recently, some doubt has been cast on the causal links of the SCP paradigm by the theory of market contestability, as developed by US economists Baumol, Panzar and Willig. A market is 'contestable' if entry to it is possible. The theory of contestability suggests that the very fact that a market is potentially open to a new entrant will serve to contain the behaviour of monopolists – i.e. market contestability prevents the exploitation of market power to restrict output and to raise prices (Lipsey and Chrystal, 1995: 271). Contestable markets are therefore said to be susceptible to 'hit and run' entry (George et al., 1992: 276).

How media firms behave, in practice, under different market structures has been a concern for many media economists (Picard, 1989: 79–83; Wirth and Bloch, 1995; Albarran, 1996) and will be a subject of interest throughout this book.

WHAT IS SO SPECIAL ABOUT THE ECONOMICS OF THE MEDIA?

Because media and other 'cultural' output have special qualities not shared by other products and services, the application of economic theory and economic perspectives in the context of media presents a variety of challenges. Media output seems to defy the very premise on which the laws of economics are based – scarcity. However much a film, a song or a news story is consumed, it does not get used up.

Economics seeks to promote 'efficiency' in the allocation of resources. The notion of economic efficiency is inextricably tied up with objectives. But the objectives of media organizations tend to vary widely. Very many media organizations comply with the classical theory of the firm and, like commercial entities in any other industry, are primarily geared towards maximizing profits and satisfying shareholders. A good number, however, appear to be driven by alternative motives. For those who operate in the public service sector, quality of output and other 'public service' type objectives form an end in themselves. Some broadcasting firms find themselves in between the market and the non-market sector – appearing to fulfil one set of objectives for an industry regulator, and another set for shareholders. Because objectives are hazy, the application of any all-embracing model based in conventional economic theory is difficult.

In free market economies, most decisions concerning resource allocation are made through the price system. But the relationship between price and resource allocation in the media is somewhat unusual, particularly in broadcasting where (notwithstanding the growth of subscription-based channels) many of the services consumers receive still do not involve a direct payment from the viewer. Without price as a direct link between consumers and producers, there is a failure in the usual means of regis-tering consumer preferences with suppliers.

In terms of economics, production methods are said to be inefficient if it would be possible to produce more of at least one commodity – without simultaneously producing less of another – merely by reallocating resources. However, when it comes to the production of media output, this approach begins to look inadequate. For example, it might well be possible for a television company to redistribute its resources so as to produce more hours of programming output or bigger audiences for the same cost as before. But if this were to narrow the diversity of media output, could it be said to be a more efficient use of resources?

These questions about the efficiency of production and allocation belong to the branch of economic theory called welfare economics. Much of the work that has been carried out in the UK in relation to broadcasting economics and associated public policy issues – most notably by Alan Peacock and, more recently, by Gavyn Davies and others – belongs to this area. Implicit in this approach is the assumption that a 'welfare function' (i.e. a functional relation showing the maximum welfare that can be generated by alternative resource decisions) can be defined for society as a whole. Within such a conceptual framework, media economics can play a role in showing how to minimize the welfare loss associated with any policy choices surrounding media provision.

KEY ECONOMIC CHARACTERISTICS OF THE MEDIA

A good way of getting to grips with what is special about media economics is to consider the characteristics of the media as a whole that distinguish it from other areas of economic activity. One such feature is that media firms often sell their wares simultaneously in two separate and distinct sorts of markets. Media industries are unusual in that they generally operate in what has been referred to by Picard as a 'dual product' market (1989: 17–19). The two commodities that media firms generate are, first, content (television programmes, newspaper copy, magazine articles, etc.) and, second, audiences. The entertainment or news content that listeners, viewers or readers 'consume' constitutes one form of output which media firms can sell. The audiences that have been attracted by this content constitute a second valuable output, insofar as access to audiences can be packaged, priced and sold to advertisers.

Audiences are the main currency for many media companies, as these provide advertising revenue which, as later chapters will discuss, is a primary source of income for commercial television and radio broadcasters as well as for newspapers and many magazines. Even non-profit-seeking media are concerned with audiences. Public service broadcasters, for example, must pay close attention to their ratings and the demographic profile of their audience because the audience utility or satisfaction they can demonstrate is normally central to negotiations surrounding what level of funding, whether public or otherwise, is made available to them.

The other type of media output – i.e. content – exhibits a number of interesting and unusual features, as have been noted by, for example, Blumler and Nossiter (1991) and Collins et al. (1988: 7–10). Media content is generally classified as a 'cultural' good. Feature films, television broadcasts, books and music are not merely commercial products but may also be appreciated for the ways they enrich our cultural environment. Many cultural goods share the quality that their value for consumers is tied up with the information or messages they convey, rather than with the material carrier of that information (the radio spectrum, CD, etc.). Messages and meanings are, of course, intangible. So media content is not 'consumable' in the purest sense of this term (Albarran, 1996: 28).

It is sometimes difficult to define what constitutes a unit of media content. This could describe, for example, a story, an article, a television programme, an entire newspaper or a radio channel. One way or another, the essential quality that audiences get value from is meanings, which are not, in themselves, material objects. Because the value of media content is generally to do with attributes that are immaterial, it does not get used up or destroyed in the act of consumption. If one person watches a television broadcast, it doesn't diminish someone else's opportunity of viewing it. Because it is not used up as it is consumed, the same content can be supplied over and over again to additional consumers.

So television and radio broadcasts exhibit one of the key features of being a 'public good'. Other cultural goods such as works of art also qualify as public goods because the act of consumption by one individual does not reduce their supply to others. Public goods contrast with normal or private goods in that private goods (such as a loaf of bread, jar of honey or pint of Guinness) *will* get used up as they are consumed. As soon as one person consumes a loaf of bread it is no longer available to anyone else. A loaf of bread can only be sold once. But when an idea or a story is sold, the seller still possesses it and can sell it over and over again.

The consumption of private goods uses up scarce resources and therefore needs to be rationed (usually by the market and by prices). But public goods do not comply with this logic. The initial cost involved in establishing a public good may be high but then the marginal costs associated with supplying an extra unit of it are next to zero. The marginal cost involved in conveying a television or radio programme to an extra viewer or listener within one's transmission reach is typically zero, at least for terrestrial broadcasters. Likewise, the marginal cost of providing an online publication to one additional Internet user is negligible.

Hoskins et al. (1997: 31–2) note the widespread use of a Research and Development (R&D) analogy to exemplify the very high initial production costs and low replication costs which are characteristic of broadcasting and other media. Generally speaking, once the first copy of a media product has been created (in the expensive R&D phase), it then costs little or nothing to reproduce and supply to extra customers. Increasing marginal returns will be enjoyed as the audience for any given media product expands.

Conversely, there are relatively few savings available for media firms when audiences contract. In most other industries, producers can vary some of their costs up and down in response to how much of their product is being sold (they can cut back on purchases of raw materials if demand slows down). For broadcasters, however, the cost of putting together and transmitting a given programme service is fixed, irrespective of how many viewers tune in or fail to tune in. Similarly, few savings can be made by newspaper and other print media publishers when circulation fails to live up to expectations (although, unlike in broadcasting, marginal print and distribution costs are present).

ECONOMIES OF SCALE

Economies of scale, then, are a highly prevalent feature of the media industry. They will be mentioned and discussed frequently throughout this book so it is worth clarifying what is meant by the term. Economies of scale are said to exist in any industry where marginal costs are lower than average costs. When the cost of providing an extra unit of a good falls as the scale of output expands, then economies of scale are present.

Many industries experience economies of scale, especially those engaged in manufacturing (e.g. of cars) where larger production runs and automated assembly line techniques lead to ever lower average production costs. A variety of reasons may explain why economies of scale are present. Sometimes it is because large firms can achieve better (bulk) discounts on required inputs than smaller firms can. Often, scale economies are to do with the benefits of specialization and division of labour that are possible within large firms.

Economies of scale exist in the media because of the public-good attributes of the industry's product. For media firms, marginal costs (MC) refer to the cost of supplying a product or service to one extra consumer. Average costs (AC) are the total costs involved in providing the product or service, divided by its audience – the total number of users who watch, read, listen to or otherwise consume it. In most sectors of the media, marginal costs tend to be low, and in some cases they are zero. Marginal costs are virtually always lower than average costs. Consequently, as more viewers tune in or more readers purchase a copy of the magazine, the average costs to the firm of supplying that product will be lowered. If average production costs go down as the scale of consumption of the firm's output increases, then economies of scale and higher profits will be enjoyed.

ECONOMIES OF SCOPE

Economies of scope are also to do with making savings and gaining efficiencies as more of a firm's output is consumed. In this case, however, savings are created by offering variations in the character or scope of the firm's output. Economies of scope – economies achieved through multi-product production – are commonly characteristic of media enterprises and, again, this is to do with the public-good nature of media output.

Economies of scope are generally defined as the economies available to firms 'large enough to engage efficiently in multi-product production and associated large scale distribution, advertising and purchasing' (Lipsey and Chrystal, 1995: 880). They arise when there are some shared overheads or other efficiency gains available that make it more cost-effective for two or more related products to be produced and sold jointly, rather than separately. Savings may arise if specialist inputs gathered for one product can be re-used in another.

Economies of scope are common in the media because the nature of media output is such that it is possible for a product created for one market to be reformatted and sold through another. For example, an interview with a politician which is recorded for broadcast in a documentary might also be edited for inclusion in other news programmes, either on television or, indeed, on radio: the same television content can be repackaged into more than one product. And the reformatting of a product intended for one audience into another 'new' product suitable for a different audience creates economies of scope.

Whenever economies of scope are present diversification will be an economically efficient strategy because 'the total cost of the diversified firm is low compared with a group of single-product firms producing the same output' (Moschandreas, 1994: 155). Strategies of diversification are increasingly common amongst media firms and this reflects the widespread availability of economies of scope. Economies of scope and economies of scale are important characteristics of the economics of media and these concepts will be developed and exemplified in later chapters.

two

CORPORATE STRATEGIES

This chapter examines the relationship between the special economic characteristics of media and the corporate configurations that media firms tend to adopt. The vertical supply chain for media is introduced and strategies of horizontal, diagonal and vertical expansion are explained. Taking account of how media markets have been altered by recent technological and regulatory changes, the advantages and benefits available to firms from strategies of monomedia (single sector) and cross-media growth are analysed.

After studying this chapter, you should be able to:

- Understand what is meant by the vertical supply chain
- Distinguish between strategies of vertical, horizontal and diagonal growth
- Discuss the implications for media firms of 'convergence' and of 'globalization'
- Explain the principal motivations behind media and cross-media expansion
- Analyse the economic advantages associated with these strategies

THE VERTICAL SUPPLY CHAIN FOR MEDIA

In order to analyse an industry, one approach used by economists is to carry out a vertical deconstruction or disaggregation. The production of any good or service usually involves several stages that are technically separable. Vertical deconstruction means breaking the industry's activities up into a number of different functions or stages so that each activity can be studied more closely. The concept behind the vertical supply chain is that the activities of an industry are ordered in a sequence which starts 'upstream' at the early stages in the production process, works its way through succeeding or 'downstream' stages where the product is processed and refined, and finishes up as it is supplied or sold to the customer.

This framework provides a useful starting point for analysing the media. For media industries, it is possible to identify a number of broad stages in the vertical supply chain which connect producers with consumers. The first is the business of creating media content (e.g. gathering news stories, or making television or radio programmes). Second, media content has to be assembled into a product (e.g. a newspaper or television service). Third, the finished product must be distributed or sold to consumers (Figure 2.1).

Essentially, the media industry is about supplying content to consumers. The aim is to make intellectual property, package it and maximize revenues by selling it as many times as is feasible to the widest possible audience and at the highest possible price. The first stage in this process is usually 'production'. The creation of media content is carried out by filmmakers, writers, journalists, musicians, television and radio production companies. Producers may sometimes supply content directly to consumers but, more generally, their output (e.g. television programmes) takes the form of inputs for a succeeding 'packaging' stage. This is when content is collected together and assembled into a marketable media product or service and it is carried out by, for example, newspaper publishers, television networks and magazine publishers. Finally there is 'distribution', which means delivering a media product to its final destination – the audience.

Distribution of media output takes place in several different ways and, for some products, is quite a complex phase. Television and radio services are generally transmitted over the airwaves or conveyed via broadband communication infrastructures. Distribution of pay-television services, however, involves encryption and subscriber management activities as well as transmission of signals. Newspapers and periodicals are usually conveyed to the consumer via another intermediary – newsagents – or they may be delivered directly to the home or to places of employment on

FIGURE 2.1   The vertical supply chain for media

a subscription basis. Electronic distribution over the Internet is another possibility for most types of media content.

All of the stages in the vertical supply chain for media are interdependent. For example, media content has no value unless it is distributed to an audience, and distribution infrastructures and outlets have no value without content to disseminate. No single stage is more important than another: all are interrelated. So, the performance of every firm involved in the supply chain will be threatened if a 'bottleneck' develops – i.e. if one player manages to monopolise any single stage in the chain. If one company gains control over all the substitute inputs at an upstream stage, or all of the facilities required for distribution, then rivals will be put at a considerable disadvantage and consumers are also likely to suffer.

The interdependent relation of different phases in the supply chain has important implications for what sort of competitive and corporate strategies media firms will choose to pursue. The desire for more control over the market environment may act as an incentive for firms to diversify into additional upstream or downstream phases. Vertical integration refers to the extent to which related activities up and down the supply chain are integrated or are carried out jointly by 'vertically integrated' firms whose activities span two or more stages in the supply process. Media firms may expand their operations vertically either by investing new resources or by acquiring other firms that are already established in succeeding or preceding stages in the supply chain.

CHANGING MARKET STRUCTURES AND BOUNDARIES

Economics provides a theoretical framework for analysing markets based on the clearly defined structures of perfect competition, monopolistic competition, oligopoly and monopoly. In practice, many media firms – especially broadcasters – have tended to operate in markets where levels of competition have been strongly influenced by technological factors (e.g. spectrum scarcity) or by state regulations (e.g. broadcasting licence requirements) or by both. These factors have held back competition. In addition, the traditional tendency for media organizations to operate in quite specific geographic markets, and to be closely linked to those markets by their product content and the advertising services they provide within those markets, has curtailed levels of domestic and international competition in some, though not all, mass-media products and services.

However, things are changing. Many of the traditional legislative and technical constraints have recently given way to more competitive market structures. In print media, new technology has reduced some of the high production costs which used to impede industry entry (Picard, 1998: 123–4). In broadcasting, a steady expansion in the means of delivery (via cable, satellite and, more recently, digital technology) has removed spectrum scarcity and opened up markets to new service providers (Brown, 1999: 17). In audiovisual production, lower capital costs of digital equipment have reduced technology-based entry barriers. And some new content creators have been successful in exploiting the distribution access offered by the growth of the Internet.

But just as new technologies and liberalizing legislation have done away with some of the conventional entry barriers affecting media markets, one or two other new barriers have sprung up in their place. The development of pay television has added extra stages to the vertical supply chain for broadcasting and some of these new stages have been particularly prone to monopolisation. In the UK, for example, ownership of the dominant encryption and conditional access technology required to charge viewers for satellite broadcasts has remained under the control of a single proprietor, News Datacom (a sister company of BSkyB). The term 'gateway monopolist' is used to describe firms that gain control over some vital stage in the supply chain or 'gateway' between the broadcaster and viewer. If left unrestrained by regulators, such gateway monopolists clearly threaten to create new entry barriers in the broadcasting sector (Cowie and Marsden, 1999).

More generally, the traditional boundaries surrounding media markets are being eroded. National markets are being opened up by what is sometimes referred to as 'globalization'.

> The communications revolution has . . . caused an internationalization of competition in almost all industries. National markets are no longer protected for local producers by high costs of transportation and communication or by the ignorance of foreign firms . . . Global competition is fierce competition, and firms need to be fast on the uptake . . . if they are to survive.
> (Lispey and Chrystal, 1995: 258)

The emergence of a borderless economy and more international competition has naturally affected media markets and firms across the globe (Carveth et al., 1998: 223). The transnational integration of markets that were previously just national markets through, for example, the European Union and North American Free Trade Agreement (NAFTA), has accelerated the process. Throughout the 1990s, policy-makers in the USA and Europe sought to develop initiatives which supported the development of a 'global information society'. To some extent at least, their hopes have been realized by the dramatic growth of a truly transnational and borderless distribution infrastructure for media in recent years – the Internet.

So, changes in technology are also helping to erode traditional market boundaries. And it is not just geographic market boundaries that are being affected but also product markets. Technological convergence has blurred the boundaries between different sorts of media and communication products and markets. The term 'convergence' is used in different ways but, generally speaking, it refers to the coming together of the technologies of media, telecommunications and computing. Digital technology – the reduction of pieces of information to the form of digits in a binary code consisting of zeros and ones – is the driving force behind convergence. Sectors of industry that were previously seen as separate are now converging or beginning to overlap because of the shift towards using common digital technologies.

The implications of convergence are far-reaching. With the arrival of common digital storage, manipulation, packaging and delivery techniques for information (in all types of media content), media output can more readily be repackaged for dissemination in alternative formats. For example, images and text gathered for a magazine, once reduced to digits, can very easily be retrieved, reassembled and delivered as another product (say, an electronic newsletter). Digitization and convergence are weakening some of the market boundaries that used to separate different media products.

Convergence is also drawing together the broadcasting, computing and information technology (IT) sectors. According to consultants KPMG, '[u]ltimately, there will be no differences between broadcasting and telecommunications' (Styles et al., 1996: 8). More and more homes are now linked into advanced high capacity communication networks and, through these, can receive a range of multimedia, interactive and other 'new' media and communication services as well as conventional television and telephony. Because of the potential for economies of scale and scope, the greater the number of products and services that can be delivered to consumers via the same communications infrastructure, the better the economics of each service.

STRATEGIC RESPONSES OF MEDIA FIRMS

The ongoing globalization of media markets and convergence in technology between media and other industries (especially telecommunications and computers) have caused many media firms to adapt their business and corporate strategies. As traditional market boundaries and barriers have begun to blur and fade away, the increase in competition amongst the media has been characterized by a steady growth in the number of perceived distributive outlets (or 'windows') which are available to media firms.

The logic of exploiting economies of scale creates an incentive to expand product sales into secondary external or overseas markets. As market structures have been freed up and have become more competitive and international in outlook, the opportunities to exploit economies of scale and economies of scope have increased. Globalization and convergence have created additional possibilities and incentives to re-package or to 'repurpose' media content into as many different formats as is technically and commercially feasible (book, magazine serializations, television programmes and formats, video, etc.) and to sell that product through as many distribution channels or windows in as many geographic markets and to as many paying consumers as possible.

The media industry's response has been marked. Media firms have been joining forces at a faster pace than ever before. They have been involved in takeovers, mergers and other strategic deals and alliances, not only with rival firms in the same business sector, but also with firms involved in other areas of the media and even with firms in other industries (e.g. tele-communications) which are now seen as complementary business areas.

Convergence and globalization have strengthened trends towards concentrated media and cross-media ownership, with the growth of integrated conglomerates (e.g. Time Warner/AOL, Pearson, Bertelsmann) whose activities span several areas of the industry. This makes sense. Highly concentrated firms who can spread production costs across wider product and geographic markets will, of course, benefit from natural economies of scale and scope in the media (Hoskins et al., 1997: 22; Corn-Revere and Carveth, 1998: 64–5). Enlarged, diversified and vertically integrated groups seem well suited to exploit the technological and other market changes sweeping across the media and communications industries.

At least three major strategies of corporate growth can be identified and distinguished: horizontal, vertical and diagonal expansion. A **horizontal** merger occurs when two firms at the same stage in the supply chain or who are engaged in the same activity combine forces. Horizontal expansion is a common strategy in many sectors: it allows firms to expand their market share and, usually, to rationalize resources and gain economies of scale. Companies that do business in the same area can benefit from joining forces in a number of ways, for example by applying common managerial techniques or finding greater opportunities for specialization of labour as the firm gets larger. In the media industry the prevalence of economies of scale makes horizontal expansion a very attractive strategy.

Vertical growth involves expanding either forward into succeeding stages or backward into preceding stages in the supply chain. Vertically integrated media firms may have activities that stretch from creation of media output (which brings ownership of copyright) through to distribution or retail of that output in various guises. Vertical expansion generally results in reduced transaction costs for the enlarged firm. Another benefit, which may be of great significance for media players, is that vertical integration gives firms some control over their operating environment and it can help them to avoid losing market access in important upstream or downstream phases.

Diagonal or 'lateral' expansion occurs when firms diversify into new business areas. For example, a merger between a telecommunications operator and a television company might generate efficiency gains as both sorts of services – audiovisual and telephony – are distributed jointly across the same communications infrastructure. Newspaper publishers may expand diagonally into television broadcasting or radio companies may diversify into magazine publishing. A myriad of possibilities exists for diagonal expansion across media and related industries. One useful benefit of this strategy is that it helps to spread risk. Large diversified media firms are, to some extent at least, cushioned against any damaging movements that affect any single one of the sectors they are involved in. More importantly perhaps, the widespread availability of economies of scale and scope means that many media firms stand to benefit from strategies of diagonal expansion.

In addition, many media firms have become what are called **transnationals** – corporations with a presence in many countries and (in some cases) a decentralized management structure. Globalization has encouraged media operators to look beyond the local or home market as a way of expanding their consumer base horizontally and of extending their economies of scale. For example, UK media conglomerate EMAP plc acquired several magazine publishing operations in France in the mid-1990s and has since expanded heavily into the US market. Swedish group Bonnier, which specializes in business news and information, expanded into the UK in autumn 2000 with the launch of a new daily newspaper, *Business AM*, in Scotland.

The basic rationale behind all such strategies of enlargement is usually to try and use common resources more fully. Diversified and large scale media organizations are clearly in the best position to exploit common resources across different product and geographic markets. Enlarged enterprises are better able to reap the economies of scale and scope which are naturally present in the industry and which, thanks to globalization and convergence, have become even more pronounced.

This leads towards what Demers calls the 'paradox of capitalism' – that increased global competition results in *less* competition in the long run (Demers, 1999: 48). Even with a loosening up of national markets and fewer technological barriers to protect media incumbents from new competitors, the trend that exists in the media – of increased concentration of ownership and power in the hands of a few very large transnational corporations – clearly reflects the overwhelming advantages that accrue to large scale firms.

MANAGERIAL THEORIES

The economic characteristics of media output and the market changes discussed above provide a compelling explanation for why profit-maximizing media firms should pursue strategies of expansion. But there are alternative schools of thought on what it is that drives firms – media or otherwise – to expand. Other approaches suggest that expansion is usually more to do with satisfying the personal interests of managers rather than with maximizing profits.

Most firms these days take the form of a public limited company (or plc) and are run by managers rather than by owners (or shareholders). Ownership and control of the firm are therefore separate and, because managers have different objectives from shareholders, a divergence from profit maximization becomes possible.

> Principal–agent analysis shows that, when ownership and control are separated, the self-interest of agents . . . [in this case, media managers] . . . will tend to make profits lower than in a 'perfect', frictionless world in which principals . . . [in this case, media shareholders] . . . act as their own agents. (Lipsey and Chrystal, 1995: 318)

Managers are, of course, concerned with keeping up profits, but they also have their own personal concerns. Marris – an influential management theorist – suggested that a principal aim of managers is try to expand the firms they are running, at all costs, and irrespective of whether it would make the firm more efficient or more profitable (Moschandreas, 1994: 284–5). The suggestion by Marris, Williamson and other managerial theorists is that growth of the firm is the main objective because this raises managerial utility 'by bringing higher salaries, power, status, and job security' (Griffiths and Wall, 1999: 91).

So the reasons why managers try to expand the firm may be because, first, salary levels for senior management are quite closely linked to the scale of a firm's activities. For example, the Chief Executive of British Telecommunications (BT) earns more than the Chief Executive of Scottish Media Group (SMG) or of the Stirling Observer. Fast-growing rather than static firms also give higher remuneration to managers. In addition, as a firm grows, its senior managers become powerful captains of industry and are often invited to join prestigious industry bodies, such as the Confederation of British Industry (CBI). The senior manager of a large media firm clearly has a powerful and politically influential role.

Another reason why managers try to 'build empires' may be because it makes it more difficult for their firm to be taken over by a predator. Senior managers usually want to avoid takeover and the risk of replacement by a new management team. By expanding – e.g. through acquisition of several smaller companies – a firm makes itself a more expensive and difficult target for takeover. The less prone a firm is to takeover, the greater the job security of its senior managers.

Most scholars of industrial economics accept that managers have some element of discretion to pursue goals other than profit maximization, and that managerial agendas can sometimes help explain corporate behaviour. On the other hand, deterministic approaches to expansion on the part of the firm tend to emphasize profit maximization as the fundamental motive. The remaining sections of this chapter draw on recent empirical research carried out in the UK for examples of what sorts of benefits and advantages accrue, in practice, as media firms expand.[1]

ADVANTAGES OF HORIZONTAL EXPANSION

In general, horizontal expansion – i.e. expansion in a firm's market share, either through internal growth or by acquisition of another firm with a similar product – may be motivated by the profit-maximizing firm's desire for greater market power (e.g. the ability to exercise some control over price) or by efficiency gains. The net impact of expansion on market performance and, ultimately, on societal welfare generally depends on the trade-off between these two possible outcomes. Whereas the achievement of efficiency gains (an improved use of resources) may be seen as serving the public interest, the accumulation of market power and market dominance may lead to behaviour and practices which run contrary to the public interest.

The relationship between the size and efficiency of firms depends largely on the availability of economies of scale: on whether marginal costs are less than average costs as output expands (Martin, 1993: 21). Economies of scale, which are frequently cited as the most important motive for

---

1. The findings of this research are reported in fuller detail in Doyle (2000).

horizontal mergers or acquisitions (Griffiths and Wall, 1999: 90–1), are a particularly prevalent incentive for expansion by media firms.

The experience of a sample of UK television broadcasting companies in 1996 provides evidence that large broadcasters are more profitable than small ones (Figure 2.2). The correlation between market share and profitability suggested by this data is largely to do with economies of scale.[2] The factors other than size which are most likely to have a bearing on the financial performance of individual media companies are variations in managerial efficiency and niche product positions. The relationship between size and performance may, of course, be subject to some additional complexities.[3] Nonetheless, the evidence provided by this sample group confirms that television broadcasters enjoy greater economies of scale (and, in turn, higher profits) as their market share expands.

This correlation is not entirely surprising. As previous writers have noted, extensive product-specific economies of scale exist in the broadcasting industry because, once a delivery infrastructure is in place, the marginal costs of providing the service to an additional viewer (within one's

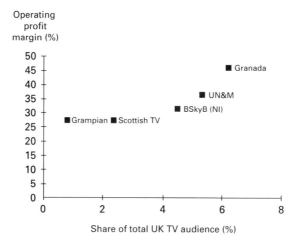

FIGURE 2.2   Market share and operating profit margins in television broadcasting in 1996

Note: Figures compiled drawing on Broadcasters Audience Research Board (BARB) ratings, company annual accounts and estimates for divisional analysis. News International (NI) is the largest shareholder in satellite broadcasting BSkyB. United News & Media (UN&M), like Granada, Scottish Television and Grampian Television operated one or more regional terrestrial services in 1996.

---

2. According to findings gathered from interviews carried out in 1997 with senior managers across this group of UK media firms.
3. Different delivery systems for television in the UK have different cost and revenue structures, partly reflecting technology but also because of (uneven) regulation.

transmission area or 'footprint') are zero or extremely low (Cave, 1989: 11–12). The overhead costs associated with providing a given service tend to be equal, regardless of audience size and so, *ceteris paribus*, economies of scale arise as larger audiences are translated into more revenue.

Economies of scale are present in virtually all sectors of the media, from magazine publishing to radio broadcasting to music publishing. Consequently, horizontal expansion is an advantageous strategy for most media firms. In newspaper publishing, for example, the marginal costs involved in selling one additional copy of the same edition of a newspaper are relatively low, so product-specific economies of scale will arise as circulations expand. Marginal costs are positive since (unlike broadcasting) the product is delivered in a tangible form, involving some printing and distribution costs. But editorial overheads tend to be the largest single component of expenditure for print media publishers and these do not necessarily change as consumption of the product expands or contracts. The editorial overheads associated with publishing any given newspaper title tend to be 'fixed', regardless of actual circulation volume, and so economies of scale can be gained as larger levels of readership are translated into more revenue.

The widespread availability of economies of scale in the media industry is generally associated with low replication costs for media output. Initial production costs (the cost of creating the first or master copy) may be high but then very few marginal costs are incurred as the product is replicated and distributed or sold over and over again to ever greater numbers of consumers. However, even within the expensive initial content production phase, economies of scale may be present. Firms engaged in content production may find that marginal costs (say, the cost of creating one additional hour of a television drama) are lower than average costs (total production costs divided by the number of hours of drama already produced) as output expands.

As the output of a television production company increases, the firm may derive economies of scale on fixed overheads by, for example, making better use of capital equipment (cameras, post-production facilities, etc.) or salaried personnel. So horizontal expansion may be motivated by the desire to increase the use of under-utilized resources. Media companies that expand horizontally and increase their output may also enjoy productivity gains because of the opportunity for specialization of tasks as the firm grows larger. The realization of scale economies may, arguably, facilitate higher levels of gross investment and speedier adoption of new technologies on the part of large media firms. And faster growing media firms may be able to attract better-quality personnel.

When a firm expands horizontally, an important potential efficiency gain is the opportunity to spread the use of specialized resources or expertise across more than one product. Any savings made in this way represent economies of scope. Efficiency gains will arise if specialist content gathered for one media product can be re-used in another.

So economies of scope as well as economies of scale may co-exist for television broadcasters who operate more than one programme service, and the more homogeneity possible between both services, the greater the economies of scope. To the extent that the owner of two regional broadcasting services or two local cable franchises is able to share the same programming, or common elements of programming, a cost advantage can be achieved. Broadcasting 'networks', which are discussed in Chapter 4, are based on the logic of exploiting such advantages. As a broadcaster expands horizontally and increases the number of services it is delivering, opportunities arise to combine back-office activities (e.g. finance and administration) as well as specialist support functions such as airtime sales or secondary programme sales.

The prevalence of economies of scope in the media explains the widespread tendency towards expansion and the high number of multi-product firms. For example, EMAP plc currently owns some 19 separate local radio stations throughout the UK. News Corporation owns four major national newspaper titles.

For newspaper proprietors that publish more than one title, various economies of scope may arise. Large publishers may achieve better collective terms on input prices or support services (e.g. printing or distribution). Publishers of several titles may be able to combine and rationalize back-office functions or other shared activities such as advertising sales. However, there is disagreement about the extent to which economies of scope can be gained within the editorial process. Perspectives offered by experienced managers in the UK newspaper industry indicate a divergence in opinions about how far the process of sharing costs between different newspaper titles can go.

At one extreme, some newspaper executives believe that the most cost-effective way to produce a given range of titles is to draw, as appropriate to each newspaper's individual character, on what is regarded as a completely flexible internal pool of shared journalistic expertise:

> [Title X] . . . has a whole machinery for covering television soap operas and the Royal Family, so why would it be duplicated by . . . [Title Y]?
>
> Why doesn't . . . [Title Y] simply *leverage* the resource brought in by its partner newspaper, and customise it, so that it's all in the editing process rather than the gathering process?[4]

---

4. Citation from interview carried out in April 1997 with the CEO of a major UK newspaper publishing firm.

However, many publishers are sceptical about the benefits available from trying to integrate as many cost functions as possible for competing titles. Combining the journalistic functions of different titles may yield cost savings but a majority of UK publishers seem to feel that this would jeopardize the individual tone of each product:

> We've looked at all this and it is not any easy one . . . Sharing journalists across different titles would be extreme. It is *very* hard to do . . . You risk losing the independence of your title . . .[5]

The presence of economies of scale and scope in the media implies a natural gravitation towards oligopoly market structures and large scale multi-product firms. Provided that product quality does not suffer as a result of sharing or spreading costs amongst more consumers or over a greater number of media products, then strategies of horizontal expansion will yield efficiency gains which, in theory, ought to add to societal welfare. However, if cost-savings are achieved at the expense of viewers' or readers' utility then we cannot say that expansion leads to improved efficiency.

Aside from efficiency, another important advantage of having a large market presence in any sector of the media (or of cross-owning media products in several sectors) is that it gives the firm greater 'critical mass'. Large firms have greater negotiating leverage in deals with suppliers and with buyers. For example, large newspaper and magazine publishers will tend to get a better deal on paper and newsprint prices. A dominant firm has greater ability to exercise some control over the prices it charges its customers. Large media firms who control access to mass audiences may well be able to command premium prices for advertising (i.e. a higher cost per thousand – CPT – rate than smaller firms).

The greater market power which large media firms command will enhance their profitability, but it may also harm consumer interests (e.g. if prices charged are too high) and it may pose a threat to the operation of markets. To the extent that the exercise of market power by large media groups serves to impede competition, then the strategic advantage it confers upon the individual firm is simultaneously an obstacle to market efficiency and a disadvantage for consumers. In summary then, strategies of horizontal expansion can deliver a range of efficiency gains that contribute positively to societal welfare but they will pose a threat when individual firms are allowed to acquire excessive market power.

5. Citation from interview carried out in April 1997 with the Finance Director of a major UK newspaper publisher and television broadcaster.

ADVANTAGES OF DIAGONAL EXPANSION

Diagonal expansion refers to developing the business sideways or 'diagonally' into what may be perceived as complementary activities (e.g. newspapers plus magazines, or television plus radio). Many strategies of diagonal cross-media expansion result in positive synergies and efficiency gains. A very important potential advantage is the opportunity to spread the use of specialized resources or expertise across more than one sort of media product. This will, of course, give rise to economies of scale and of scope.

The combinations of cross-media ownership that yield the most significant economic efficiencies tend to be those which enable the firm to share either common specialized forms of content or a common distribution infrastructure. When a media firm's output is characterized by a particular theme or subject matter, then expanding operations into several different sectors will usually create important synergies. For example, Pearson's specialization in providing one particular form of media content – management information – enables it to exploit economies of scale and scope across several different products (e.g. the *Financial Times* newspaper, FT business magazines, FT newsletters, FT newscasts, etc.) and modes of delivery (e.g. print, broadcast) for that content.

A focus on one particular type of content may enable the firm to build very strong brands that are more likely to be successful in crossing over from one platform to another. So specialization and the development of recognizable brands (e.g. the *Financial Times*) make it easier for firms to exploit new vehicles for delivery of media content, such as the Internet. In addition, diversified media companies such as Pearson or Time Warner are able to reduce costs by exploiting overlaps in the production process for some of their products. Cross-ownership between, for example, newspaper publishing, magazine publishing and book publishing creates potential economies in any processes and inputs which are common to all of these activities, such as printing and purchasing paper.

Most significantly, however, the availability of economies of scale and scope depends on the extent to which specialist inputs – i.e. elements of media content – or other important resources can be re-used or exploited more fully as the firm expands diagonally. This, in turn, may depend on how homogeneous the content of each media product is and how readily such content can be repackaged into different formats (i.e. the relationship between the marginal costs of reformatting content and the marginal revenues likely to be raised by selling it again in extra product markets).

Digitization makes it possible to reduce all sorts of images, sounds and text to a common format and to transport these via a common distribution infrastructure. Media content, when reduced to digital 'metadata', can be stored, retrieved, manipulated, reformatted and repackaged with much greater ease than before. So the spread of digital technologies across different sectors of the media and communications industries has significant implications for the savings and efficiency gains that are potentially available via strategies of diagonal cross-media expansion.

The benefits and advantages of diagonal expansion involving media and telecommunications companies have been analysed by Albarran and Dimmick, who use the term 'economies of multiformity' to describe the benefits of diagonal concentrations of ownership (1996: 43). Economies of multiformity refer to any and all advantages that firms derive from cross-owning activities in more than one sector of the media or communications industry. Such economies will be gained by a telephone company moving into the cable television industry and using its existing distribution infrastructure to sell two services instead of just one – i.e. economies of scale in distribution. Or economies of multiformity arise when the same media content is repackaged or repurposed into different media products – i.e. economies of scope. Thus, the term 'economies of multiformity' embraces all benefits that come about through diagonal cross-ownership in the media and communications industries.

Different combinations of diagonal cross-ownership will, of course, yield different sorts of efficiency gains. Expansion from print to electronic publishing offers plentiful opportunity to share or repurpose specialist content between these two different text-based activities. Likewise, diagonal mergers between magazine and newspaper publishers can offer operational synergies. Efficiency gains are also possible, to some extent, through sharing of production and transmission resources between radio and television (as exemplified by the 'bi-media' approach introduced at the BBC in the 1990s).

However, combinations of text-based plus audio products, or text-based plus audiovisual products will not necessarily give rise to economies of scale or scope or to any other economic advantages. Where a newspaper and a television service share a strong common focus or theme (e.g. a focus on business news or on a specific locality) then clearly opportunities will arise to share or repurpose intellectual property. But when no such overlap in content exists then relatively few other potential efficiency gains seem to be available. Some opportunities may arise to combine back-office activities or, perhaps, to introduce improvements in managerial efficiency but no more than in any merger involving other (loosely related) sectors of activity. As one senior UK media executive points out:

> [t]here are actually a lot of successful groups who have operated both [television broadcasting and newspaper publishing], always operating each *distinctly* – with the exception of, occasionally, slavishly cross-promoting [e.g. using an established newspaper title to promote a new TV service] . . .

> I do not think that television and newspapers are a 'natural' diversification from each other.

Notwithstanding the spread of digital technologies, the skills, techniques and equipment involved in newspaper production and distribution are, in fact, generally still quite *different* from those required in the television industry, and vice versa. So, combining these activities under common ownership will not necessarily create any special efficiency gains or opportunities to rationalize resources. Unless each service has a strong shared focus there is little economic incentive for seeking to combine these activities. Consequently, diversified media conglomerates such as News Corporation will often allow broadcasting and newspaper subsidiaries to operate in almost complete isolation from each other.

If 'natural' economies of scope between broadcasting and newspaper publishing activities are non-existent, it follows that few economic benefits can be directly or solely attributed to diagonal expansion from television to newspapers or vice versa. Why then, are strategies of diagonal cross-media ownership so common?

One very important special feature of cross-owning television and newspapers is the opportunity it creates to cross-promote the firm's products. Whether this feature is economically beneficial or damaging depends on how it is used. When cross-promotion is used to facilitate *de novo* expansion (the introduction of new products which increase choice) then welfare and competition should be enhanced (Moschandreas, 1994: 349). For example, if a media conglomerate uses the pages of its newspapers to attract attention to and promote the launch of a new television service that adds to competition and viewer choice then, arguably, cross-promotion is economically beneficial. On the other hand, if the conglomerate uses cross-promotion to build cross-sectoral dominance for its existing media products then this will have a negative impact on competition and on pluralism.

Risk-reduction is another potential benefit associated with diagonal expansion. Firms diversify in order to spread their risks and so that they are not too dependent on any one product market. A media firm whose income is derived wholly from advertising (e.g. a commercial radio broadcaster) may expand operations into another media sector where revenues come directly from consumers in order to protect or cushion itself against cyclical downturns in advertising expenditure. A firm operating in a declining industry may wish to diversify into a perceived growth area. The UK national newspaper industry provides a clear example of a sector which is in slow decline while subscription television and electronic media are perceived as growth areas. So newspaper publishers might well seek to diversify in order to secure growth in future earnings.

Another motivation underlying strategies of cross-media expansion is the desire to exploit anticipated synergies and 'economies of multiformity' between newspaper publishing and television broadcasting which may develop over the long term. The expectation that growth in electronic communications will stimulate demand for new products based on both audiovisual images and text has been cited as one factor encouraging diagonal mergers between UK television broadcasters and newspaper publishing companies.

Motives other than profit maximization – i.e. managerial motives – may also play a role in cross-media mergers. A television company may decide to join forces with a newspaper publishing firm as 'a defensive move' against hostile takeover, i.e. in order to make the enlarged company less attractive to potential predators. Alternatively, the managers of a media firm may pursue a strategy of diagonal expansion because, irrespective of efficiency implications, their own prestige (and, perhaps, political influence) will increase as their 'empire' grows.

So in analysing the gains that arise from any strategy of diagonal expansion, it is worth distinguishing between different sorts of advantage – efficiency gains versus risk-spreading, etc. – and between different potential beneficiaries – the firm's shareholders, or its managers or society at large. The achievement of efficiency gains (e.g. economies of scale and scope) will not only serve the interests of the firm but should also contribute to the wider good of the economy by engendering an improved use of resources. However, strategies of cross-media expansion that yield no efficiency gains and are predicated solely on the strategic interests of the firm's shareholders or managers will not give rise to any general economic gains.

On the contrary, the accumulation of greater size, more market power and dominant market positions can lead to behaviour and practices which run contrary to the public interest (Moshandreas, 1994: 483–4). Once a firm achieves a dominant position, the removal of competitive pressures may give rise to various inefficiencies, including excessive expenditure of resources aimed simply at maintaining dominance. Hence, competition policy – which applies to media as well other firms – strives to promote sufficient competition to induce firms to operate efficiently. Public policy issues surrounding concentrated media ownership are dealt with in fuller detail in Chapter 9.

ADVANTAGES OF VERTICAL EXPANSION

The vertical supply chain outlined in Figure 2.1 indicates how it is possible to break down into stages each of the activities involved in making and then supplying a media product to the consumer. For instance, the newspaper industry can be disaggregated into news-gathering, editing, printing, distribution and retailing. The television industry can be broadly broken down into programme production, assembling the schedule and transmission to viewers. Many media firms are vertically integrated – i.e. they are involved in activities at more than one stage in the supply process. Vertical expansion is a strategy which is increasingly common, for example, amongst the main US television broadcasting networks and their suppliers and rivals (Owen and Wildman, 1992: 202–4).

Why is vertical integration an attractive strategy? Broadly speaking, it makes sense to control both content production and distribution because the greater the distribution of your output the lower your per-unit production costs will be. In television, per-viewer production costs can be reduced by 'selling' the same output to as many different audiences or segments of the audience as possible. As a distributor, vertical expansion upstream into production means that you have an assured supply of appropriate content to disseminate through your distribution infrastructure. As a content producer, vertical integration with a distributor means assured access to audiences.

Vertical expansion is not only about maximizing revenues and gaining more security or control over the market. Another advantage is that it can reduce 'transaction costs'. Broadcasters who internalize the programme production process rather than purchasing programme rights in the open market may face fewer complications, delays and so on in securing exactly the sort of content they require.

So, as with other forms of expansion, the two main incentives associated with vertical growth are improved efficiency and the accumulation of market power. In any example of vertical expansion, both motives may be present and, indeed, 'the two are not unrelated' (George et al., 1992: 65). Vertical integration may be motivated by the desire to minimize costs or by the desire for greater security (e.g. access to essential raw materials such as, for a broadcaster, attractive television programming) but then the latter – the desire to gain some control over the market environment – may itself result in market dominance.

Looking more closely at how vertical integration can help minimize costs, an important consideration is the difference between the expenses involved in buying from or selling to other firms – obtaining information, negotiating contracts, etc. – and the expenses involved in carrying out the functions performed by these other firms within one's own organization.

Ronald Coase (1937) first introduced the idea that 'the market' and 'the firm' represent alternative modes for allocating resources. For Coase, firms exist because the co-ordination of economic activity through the firm (by hierarchies of managers) is less costly than through the market (by the pricing system). Integration of activities within the structure of a firm will occur because it creates 'transaction cost' savings and these act as an incentive to integrate vertically.

The potential for cost reduction within a firm may stem from improved information – about price or product specifications or, more generally, about the market. In the television industry, for example, the costs (created by uncertainty, weaker informational flows, etc.) involved in inter-firm trade between programme producers and broadcasters may well be higher than when both activities are carried out in house. It may save time and hassle to be able to source the programmes that are needed directly from an in-house production division rather than having to shop around, negotiate and make deals with external programme-makers.

But, for media firms, a more important factor encouraging vertical expansion stems from the interdependent relation of different phases in the supply chain. Media content is no good without access to audiences, and vice versa. So, the main driving force for firms to diversify into additional upstream or downstream phases is the desire to gain more security and control over the market environment. Integrated media firms can avoid the market power of dominant suppliers or buyers. Vertical expansion gives secure access to essential inputs or essential distribution outlets for output. This is a key advantage in the media, since firms depend on getting access both to content and to avenues for distribution of content.

A broadcaster that has to rely on external producers to supply all the 'hit' programmes in its schedule will find itself vulnerable to the possibility of post-contractual opportunistic behaviour on the part of these suppliers. If the supplier of a key programme series in a broadcaster's schedule threatens to withdraw that series or sell it at a higher price to a rival broadcaster, then high costs may have to be incurred to retain that programme. Vertical integration is a way of avoiding the higher costs associated with such behaviour (Martin, 1993: 274).

If monopoly power is present in the programme production stage (say, because a supplier has control over a specific programme for which no perceived substitutes are available) then, even without vertical integration, the firm with upstream monopoly power may be able to appropriate some of any monopoly profits available at the broadcasting stage (Moschandreas, 1994: 417). It is rarely the situation that no substitutes are available for a particular product but, in television programming specificity of inputs (particular actors, writers or presenters) is a factor in their popularity and success. So, to avoid being held to ransom by important suppliers, broadcasters and other media distributors may have no choice other than to expand vertically into production.

From a content-producer's point of view there are also numerous attractions in vertical integration. Ownership of, say, a broadcaster or a video distributor ensures that the firm's output will find its way to audiences. Vertical integration may lead to a more predictable and reliable stream of orders. According to the Finance Director of a major television company which is part of the ITV network in the UK, a production company that is vertically integrated with a broadcaster will gain informational advantages over its independent rivals which help it to secure more 'commissions' or orders for programmes:

> Everyone likes to pretend that there's a level playing field in terms of access [for independent and vertically integrated producers] to the ITV network – I don't think anyone actually *does* believe that because it's perfectly obvious that if you've got the same people working in production as broadcasting then you're not going to have 'Chinese Walls'. There's going to be occasions when someone from broadcasting says to someone from production – 'I'll tell you what we really want: a cracking entertainment programme for Wednesday nights'. There is absolutely no doubt that being part of ITV [broadcasting] gets the intelligence to you faster. It would be daft to pretend otherwise, because it's self-evident, really . . .

A steady and predictable production slate is an important advantage for programme-makers. This, in turn, allows the vertically integrated production company to plan more effectively and to use its production resources, equipment, technicians and personnel more efficiently. The assured distribution enjoyed by a vertically integrated production firm also helps to build that producer's reputation, or brand name, as a supplier of programmes.

An example of another sort of vertical/diagonal merger in the media industry was provided recently by Time Warner and America Online (AOL). Time Warner, a major producer of news and entertainment, owns a huge library of media content and also runs the second-largest US cable network. America Online is the largest Internet Service Provider (ISP) in the US with some 26 million subscribers. The potential gains for Time Warner/AOL from bringing together strengths both in content creation and in online distribution are clearly very promising. The dangers posed to rivals by allowing such a powerful vertically integrated entity to take shape were summed up in a *Financial Times* editorial as follows: 'The combined group could harm other content providers by restricting access to AOL subscribers and damage other ISPs by denying them access to Time Warner content' (2001: 22).

It is sometimes difficult to disentangle the pursuit of greater efficiency and greater security from the pursuit of monopoly power (George et al., 1992: 72). A media firm might well expand vertically in order to gain greater security, but the more control it acquires over all stages in the vertical supply chain, the more danger there is that it will start to dominate the market, with detrimental consequences for rivals and consumers. Vertical integration may protect the market power of incumbent firms by raising barriers to entry. For example, if all the best programme-producers are cross-owned by broadcasters then, in order to secure its own supply of attractive programming, a new market entrant in the broad-casting arena would also be forced to adopt a vertically integrated structure (thus pushing up the costs of market entry). So, vertical expansion can be seen, in one way (i.e. that of Coase), as a response to market failures and imperfections and, in another sense, as a source of such market imperfections.

three

ECONOMICS OF ADVERTISING

One of the main sources of revenue for many media organizations is advertising. Consequently, patterns of advertising activity exert a very significant influence on the fortunes of the media industry as a whole. This chapter is concerned with the key arguments surrounding the economic role played by advertising, and with its impact on market structures and on consumer decision-making. It introduces you to the economic forces and factors which determine the extent of advertising activity in an economy, examining why levels of advertising vary from one country to another, and over time. It also considers the impact of new media technologies on patterns of advertising.

After studying this chapter, you should be able to:

- Understand why advertising takes place
- Identify and explain the factors which influence the amount of advertising activity taking place in an economy, and understand why it is cyclical
- Assess whether advertising is a beneficial or a harmful economic force
- Explain the problems firms face in deciding how much of their resources to devote to advertising

THE ADVERTISING INDUSTRY

Advertising is ubiquitous. Its roots can be traced back to the cave but, in the twenty-first century, its reach and influence have become virtually inescapable. Over the last 50 years an increased willingness on the part of firms to invest in building awareness of themselves and of their wares has given rise to the rapid development of the advertising, marketing and public relations sectors. Advertising agencies have generated catchphrases, jingles and images to make brands familiar to audiences both across the globe and across generations.

Advertising is big business, and the industry it has spawned has grown quickly and diversified to keep pace with ongoing market changes and with the development of newer forms of media. Alongside the basic function of creating advertising messages, many agencies offer an array of specialist communication services, including provision of sophisticated market research information or consultancy related to sponsorship deals. The major advertising agencies in the world – of which WPP, Omnicom and Interpublic are currently the largest – are diversified multinational corporations with networks of operating subsidiaries and strategic alliances that provide clients with global audience reach as well as creative advertising ideas.

As advertising expenditure has grown in response to rising economic prosperity in the developed world, the advertising industry has flourished. According to estimates from Zenith Media (cited in Tomkins, 2000), global expenditure on advertising reached some $330 billion in the year 2000 – a sizeable slice of our collective resources. But even this understates the extent of advertising, because industry projections tend to focus on conventional media only – i.e. television, radio, press, cinema and 'outdoor' or billboard sites. This excludes some significant investment in other forms of advertising and marketing including, of growing importance since the late 1990s, expenditure on Internet advertising. It is suggested that around $7.5 billion was spent globally on Net advertising in 1999 (Zenith Media, 2001: 115) and expenditure on it is continuing to expand rapidly, particularly in the USA.

The growth of the advertising sector has brought about the establishment of various industry bodies including, in the UK, the Advertising Association (AA). Founded in 1924, the AA represents all branches of the industry and its functions include promoting the benefits of advertising, lobbying on behalf of its members and gathering information about all aspects of advertising (Meech, 1999: 29). Annual statistics compiled by the Association provide a clear picture of the extent of advertising activity both within individual sectors, such as television or radio, and across the media as a whole. The breakdown provided in Table 3.1 reveals a healthy pattern of growth in UK expenditure on advertising in all the major media in recent years.

TABLE 3.1 Breakdown of total advertising expenditure in the UK (£bn)

	1995	1996	1997	1998	1999
Press	5.98	6.41	6.97	7.53	7.83
Television	3.14	3.39	3.70	4.03	4.32
Outdoor & Transport	0.41	0.47	0.55	0.61	0.65
Radio	0.30	0.34	0.39	0.46	0.52
Cinema	0.07	0.07	0.09	0.10	0.12
Total	9.89	10.68	11.70	12.73	13.44

Source: Advertising Association (2000: 33)

WHY DOES ADVERTISING TAKE PLACE?

Why does all this advertising take place? Firms spend money on advertising in the hope of persuading consumers to buy their products. The general aim behind advertising expenditure is to try to increase sales and to reinforce consumers' loyalty to particular brands.[1] So, advertising is a form of competitive behaviour: it is one of the main tools that firms can use to compete to entice consumers to switch to their own product rather than that of a rival. Other tactics a firm might use to try to gain advantage over its competitors include making changes to the quality of the product so as to increase its attractiveness, or simply making adjustments to its price so as to undercut rivals.

According to the economic theory of firms, whether or not an organization is likely to engage in competitive behaviour depends on which kind of market structure it is operating within. As discussed earlier, the term 'competitive market structure' describes the kind of market situation a firm can find itself in, and is primarily to do with how many rivals it has, whether the market is open to new entrants, how similar the goods on offer are, and how much power each firm has in relation to market demand and over prices. Advertising generally takes place in market situations where firms have an incentive to engage in some form of competitive behaviour (Chiplin and Sturgess, 1981; Lipsey and Chrystal, 1995: 259).

Broadly speaking, the more competition that is present in a market, the greater the need to advertise. Thanks to globalization, most sectors of industry are now operating in a much more competitive environment than at any time in the past. In addition, deregulation and the wider

1. When advertising is successful, it may cause the demand curve to shift outwards (reflecting an increased market share) and also to become steeper (as price elasticity is reduced). The concept of elasticity is discussed in further detail in Chapter 7.

availability of inexpensive technological know-how have served to inten-sify competitive pressures in many areas of industry. Consequently, there is an ever-increasing trend for firms to regard advertising as the best means of differentiating and drawing attention to their own brands, and this is reflected by growth in overall levels of advertising in recent years. As demonstrated in Table 3.1 , total expenditure on advertising across the major media in the UK grew from £9.9 billion in 1995 to £13.4 billion in 1999.

Nonetheless, the decision by specific firms about whether or not to engage in advertising or other sorts of competitive behaviour is deter-mined, to a large extent, by which kind of market structure the company is operating within. Perhaps surprisingly, firms that operate in 'perfectly' competitive markets do not need to compete actively to stoke up demand for their own product because, in theory, none has any influence over the market. It is assumed that in the rather utopian circumstances of perfect competition, there is no point in any individual firm spending money to advertise its wares because each firm's goods are exactly the same as everyone else's and consumers are perfectly well aware of this.

At the other end of the scale, in very uncompetitive market circum-stances such as a monopoly or a monopolistic market structure – where there are no close substitutes for an organization's products – the firm has no rivals to worry about. So, monopolists also have relatively little to gain from expending resources on advertising.

On the other hand, firms operating in an oligopoly market structure are strongly motivated to advertise. Oligopolists do, indeed, have a degree of market power but they are aware that their rivals also have some power to influence the market. So competitive behaviour – e.g. advertising or price competition – is a particular feature of oligopolistic market struc-tures. In the real world, a very great and increasing number of industries operate in imperfectly competitive or oligopoly situations. So, at the most basic level, it is the competitive behaviour of firms operating in oligopoly market structures that fuels advertising activity. And as global competi-tion continues to intensify, patterns of advertising expenditure will reflect this trend.

ARE FIRMS IN CONTROL OF THEIR OWN MARKETS?

US economist J.K. Galbraith has put forward an interesting theory about the role of advertising. He suggests that firms use advertising to control their own markets (Lipsey and Chrystal, 1995: 321). Galbraith points out that firms have to make sizeable investments in developing and launching new products but, despite market research, they cannot be entirely certain how well these new products will be appreciated by consumers and how profitable they will turn out to be. Firms are exposed to and threatened by the unpredictability of future events, especially changes in patterns of demand or fashions or technology. So, to make the future less unpredictable, firms invest vast sums of money in advertising.

According to Galbraith, expenditure on advertising is intended to manipulate market demand and to guard against sudden unexpected shifts in public tastes. Advertising expenditure enables companies to sell what they themselves want to produce rather than what consumers would want to buy. At the same time, firms decide not to produce some new products that consumers might actually like to buy. This allows them to cut the risks and expenses involved in launching untried products which, even if they are successful, might well simply undermine the market for existing products.

So, from Galbraith's point of view, consumers appear to be the hapless victims of corporations. We are forced, by the manipulative power of advertising, to buy things we do not necessarily want and we are deprived of those products we might like to have. Can this really be true?

Even though the purpose underlying firms' expenditure on advertising is to try to increase demand for particular products, wholly unexpected shifts in consumer demand sometimes occur. At times, the demand for new categories of products or services cannot just be explained by manipulative advertising; it has to do with more basic changes, or with some technological innovation. For example, the general success of the motor car or of the washing machine can hardly be put down to brainwashing by advertisers, even if advertising may persuade us to opt for one brand of these products rather than another. Likewise, the explanation for escalating interest in Internet services in recent years seems to owe more to technology, consumer convenience and fashion than to the efforts of advertisers. So, although advertising plays an important part in shaping demand, the view that firms can effectively control their own markets is not entirely a convincing one.

Where advertising seems to be most effective is in shifting and determining the pattern of demand among existing products which are similar to each other. In other words, advertising is likely to have more of a bearing on which *brands* rather than which *products* consumers will want to buy. It undoubtedly helps to create and sustain loyalty to particular brands but it is unable to dictate overall trends in consumer demand, nor can it hope to overcome the influence of technology, fashion or the media on the sorts of products people express a wish for.

INFORMATIVE VERSUS PERSUASIVE ADVERTISING

Advertising has two related aspects: it sets out to inform consumers of the characteristics of the various products available, and it tries to influence consumers by altering their tastes or preferences and, hence, their purchasing decisions. Informative advertising – giving consumers more information about what is available to them – can be seen as playing a useful role in making the market system work more effectively. It fulfils a valuable function in facilitating the interaction of consumers and producers. The second function – persuasion – is more questionable in terms of its impact on consumer welfare.

The distinction between information and persuasion has been a major preoccupation in historic texts devoted to the economics of advertising. To summarize briefly, those who see advertising as being informative in nature tend to view it as a necessary expenditure that keeps markets competitive in a world where imperfect knowledge is a fact of life. They argue that, if we didn't have advertising, then the transaction costs (i.e. all of the costs involved in negotiating and completing a deal) of any sale or purchase – especially those to do with the search for goods and for knowledge about their attributes – would be higher and, as a result, buyers would be worse off. Not only would they have to pay more for their goods and services, but the probability of their making a wrong choice would be increased. The greater the variety of goods and services offered for sale, the more difficult it is for the consumer to judge the capacity of the good to satisfy a particular want before he or she buys it and the more the consumer will value objective information to help him or her to make the right choice.

Not surprisingly, many who work in the advertising industry take the view that advertising helps people to make choices in an over-supplied world. But if the information provided by advertising is not objective, then the choices it engenders may not be good ones and the effect of advertising will be to diminish rather than to enhance the overall welfare or utility of consumers. Those who view advertising as being primarily persuasive regard it as leading to excessive differentiation of products, resulting in prices and profits higher than those arising in an ideal competitive world (Chiplin and Sturgess, 1981: 74–7). Think, for example, of the amount Coca-Cola and Pepsi spend on advertising when, arguably, there is relatively little difference between their products. Those who argue that too many resources are being allocated to advertising are, to some extent, saying that consumers are being bombarded with rather too much information and that it pays firms to advertise beyond the point at which the advertising messages provide any benefit to consumers. They are also suggesting that the persuasive spin put upon product information by advertisers results in incomplete, misleading or distorted messages rather than a useful resource for consumers.

Is advertising generally harmful or beneficial to the operation of markets? On the one hand, consumers have to pay a higher price for products to cover the cost of advertising but, on the other, they benefit from widespread information about the range and availability of competing goods and services, and this facilitates their decision-making. In its role as a source of information for consumers, advertising can be a pro-competitive force leading to an improved allocation of resources. Counteracting such a force, however, is a possible anti-competitive effect caused by the use of advertising as a means of preventing potential rivals from gaining entry to markets.

ADVERTISING AS A BARRIER TO MARKET ENTRY

An important criticism of advertising relates to its effect on competitive market structures. It is suggested that firms use advertising to put up barriers to market entry which prevent other firms from competing with them (Chiplin and Sturgess, 1981: 112). The basic argument here is that the millions of pounds invested every year in building up recognition for their brands by, for example, Procter & Gamble, Kellogg's or Elida Fabergé make it difficult or impossible for potential new entrants to encroach on their product markets unless they also have the scale of resources and the will to match this expenditure. In other words, heavy advertising is a means of imposing high set-up costs on new entrants and this, in turn, serves to deter would-be rivals.

Advertising is a feature of oligopoly market structures. Oligopolists not only have to worry about competing with their existing rivals to build and defend market share, they also have to worry about potential competition from firms that might be tempted to enter their industry. If there are no natural barriers to entry, oligopolist firms will earn pure profits just in the short run and until such time as other firms enter their industry. Oligopolists can protect their profitability in the long run only if they can find ways of creating barriers that prevent entry.

One method of keeping out potential new entrants is called 'brand proliferation' (Lipsey and Chrystal, 1995: 269). Differentiated products – i.e. products that are similar but with some discernible differences in their attributes – usually have several characteristics that can be varied over a wide range. Thus, there is room in the market for a large number of similar products each with a somewhat different range of features or characteristics. Consider, for example, the current range of breakfast cereals or cars. Although the multiplicity of brands that manufacturers make available is, undoubtedly, at least partly a response to consumers' tastes, it may also be partly the result of a deliberate attempt by existing players to discourage the entry of new firms. When existing suppliers sell a wide array of differentiated products this makes it difficult for a new firm to gain entry on a small scale. Brand proliferation means that, in effect, all the potential niches are already occupied. The larger the number of differentiated products already being sold by existing oligopolists, the smaller the market available to a new firm entering with a single new product.

Alternatively, existing firms can create barriers to entry by imposing on new entrants significant fixed costs associated with setting up operations in that market. This is an important tactic if there are no economies of large-scale production to provide 'natural' barriers to entry. Advertising is one means by which existing firms can impose heavy set-up costs on new entrants (Griffiths and Wall, 1999: 127). Advertising, of course, has effects other than creating barriers to entry. As discussed above, it may perform the useful function of informing buyers of their alternatives. Indeed, a new firm may find it necessary to advertise even if existing firms don't bother, simply to call attention to its entry into an industry.

Nonetheless, advertising can operate as a potent entry barrier. Effective brand-image advertising means that a new firm will have to advertise in order to catch the public's attention. If the firm's sales are small then advertising costs per unit sold will be large (Lipsey and Chrystal, 1995: 270). Unit costs will only be reduced sufficiently to make a new entrant profitable when sales volumes are large, so that the fixed advertising costs needed to break into the market are spread over a large number of units.

The combined use of brand proliferation and of heavy advertising sometimes acts as a formidable entry barrier. This explains why some of the biggest advertisers often sell multiple brands of the same product. For example, amongst the top 20 advertisers in the UK in 1999 were washing powder manufacturers Procter & Gamble and Lever Brothers; shampoo manufacturers L'Oréal Golden, Van den Bergh and Elida Fabergé; car manufacturers Renault, Vauxhall, Ford, Volkswagen and Peugeot; and breakfast cereal manufacturers Kellogg's and Nestlé Rowntree (Advertising Association, 2000: 227).

To some extent, the debate about advertising and market structures is not really about the effects of advertising *per se* since both sides agree that it can work as a powerful barrier to entry. Instead, it is about whether or not barriers to market entry are a good thing or not and whether one market structure is better than another. Competition is normally considered a prerequisite for efficiency and, therefore, open and more competitive markets seem preferable to monopolised ones. If however, by keeping rivals out of the market, advertising enables firms to increase their output and to achieve economies of large-scale production, then arguably this might serve to benefit consumers. The economies of scale created by concentration of ownership in the washing powder industry, for example, means that (provided there is sufficient competition to prevent monopoly pricing) consumers should enjoy lower product prices than would be possible under a more fragmented and competitive market structure. So, provided that firms do not become so large that they can extract monopoly profits, consumers might occasionally benefit from the anti-competitive effects of advertising (Parkin et al., 1997: 424–5).

ADVERTISING AND THE PERFORMANCE OF THE ECONOMY

In recent years a great deal of detailed analysis of advertising and economic data has been undertaken by commercial agencies for the purpose of forecasting future advertising trends. In the UK, extensive historic data is compiled and analysed by the Advertising Association each year and it provides compelling evidence of a link between levels of economic wealth and of advertising activity.

Examined over a long period of time, expenditure on advertising has tended to grow as a proportion of the national economy. Advertising expenditure can be defined in various ways, for example including or excluding production costs, new media and alternative promotional expenditures. Likewise, the performance of the economy can be defined and calculated in different ways, including by Gross Domestic Product. GDP measures the total value of all productive output in the whole economy, usually over a one year period and is probably the most widely used benchmark of general economic performance. When expenditure on advertising is calculated as a percentage of GDP, the pattern that emerges indicates that as the national economy has grown over time in real terms, advertising has not just grown in parallel, but it has grown even faster. So the amount of advertising activity in an economy is related to the size and growth rates of the economy itself, and advertising has tended to account for a progressively more significant proportion of GDP as time goes on.

The relationship between wealth and levels of advertising does not simply apply to the UK. It is also clearly observable in other developed economies and can be demonstrated by a bivariate analysis of GDP per capita (i.e. the productive output of the country divided by the number of inhabitants) and advertising expenditure per capita. As demonstrated in Figure 3.1, the pattern which emerges from international comparisons

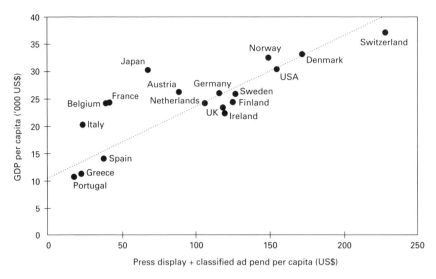

FIGURE 3.1   National advertising expenditure vs GDP, 1998
(NTC Research, Advertising Association, 2000: 22)

shows a strong and positive association between economic wealth in any country and the level of advertising expenditure it enjoys. This correlation is disturbed only occasionally when, for example, government restrictions on advertising hold back levels of expenditure on commercial airtime. Generally speaking, richer countries such as Switzerland enjoy a much higher level of advertising expenditure than poorer countries such as Greece and Portugal (Advertising Association, 2000: 22).

Why is this? There have been two arguments about the relationship between advertising and living standards. One is that advertising stimulates the levels of consumption that are found in countries with high per capita incomes. This perspective implies a causal connection between high levels of advertising, high consumption and, in turn, higher levels of economic activity and growth. The other viewpoint is that advertising is a 'waste of resources' that can only be afforded by rich countries (Chiplin and Sturgess, 1981: 7).

Historic UK data shows that the growth in advertising as a proportion of GDP is not exactly steady and continuous. Advertising growth is cyclical and it reflects, in an exaggerated way, the ups and downs of the economy at large. In periods of economic expansion the proportion of GDP spent on advertising increases; the converse is true in recession. Figure 3.2 shows advertising as a proportion of GDP over 44 years. It demonstrates how advertising, when expressed as a percentage of GDP, peaks at the top of economic boom periods such as in 1973 and 1989. By the same token, expenditure on advertising bottoms out at the lowest point in the economic

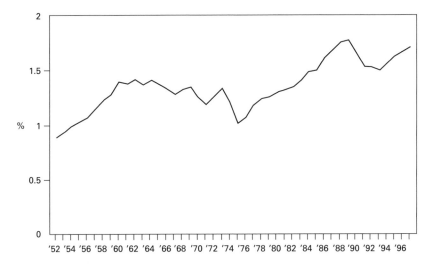

FIGURE 3.2   UK advertising as a percentage of GDP, 1952–97
(NTC Research, Advertising Association, 1998: 21)

cycle, such as in 1975 at the height of oil crisis or in the more recent recession in 1993. Advertising tends to gallop ahead more quickly than the economy in boom periods, but then slumps more quickly in recession.

To understand why advertising is cyclical, it is helpful to carry out more detailed analysis of advertising expenditure data. Advertising is sometimes broken down into 'display' and 'classified'. Display advertising (the bulk of advertising expenditure) is total advertising minus financial notices, classified and advertising in trade or technical journals. Classified is recruitment, housing, personal advertisements, etc. Different sets of factors will affect the performance of each of these two categories.

The two primary forces which appear to determine the growth or decline of display advertising expenditure are consumers' expenditure and company profits (Advertising Association, 2000: 20). The close correlation between company profits and display advertising expenditure suggests that, perhaps not surprisingly, companies can afford to and *do* spend more on advertising when times are good. Likewise, the correlation between consumers' expenditure and display advertising expenditure suggests that companies are willing to spend more when consumer spending and confidence are buoyant, i.e. when advertising expenditure is more likely to translate into increased sales. In short, advertising expenditure expands along with consumer expenditure, but is reined back when company profits are under pressure.

Classified advertising expenditure is dependent on a variety of factors, such as the state of the housing market, the second-hand car market and employment levels. Statistics published annually by the Advertising Association suggest that the level of unfilled job vacancies is a key determinant of recruitment classified expenditure (2000: 23). It is mainly recruitment advertising which pushes up classified and, thus, total advertising expenditure during economic booms.

The strength of the relationship between advertising cycles and the state of the economy has been questioned and some would argue that advertising expenditure should continue to grow, irrespective of the performance of the economy. Patrick Barwise of London Business School, for example (cited in Tomkins, 2000), suggests that advertising by firms with established brands is essentially a defensive activity, carried out in order to protect their market share rather than in the hope of boosting sales. Likewise, according to Andrew Ehrenberg of South Bank University, '[m]ost advertising is not trying to sell. It's just maintaining your position in a competitive market' (cited in Tomkins, 1999a). Be that as it may, historic trends in advertising clearly demonstrate the prevalent tendency for firms to cut back on advertising expenditure as soon as an economic downturn looms into view. As John Hegarty, Creative Director of advertising agency Bartle Bogle Hegarty, has explained: '[r]ecession is always a problem for the advertising industry, in the sense that clients feel that advertising is the first thing they can switch off' (cited in Smith, 1998: 1).

The apportionment of advertising between different sectors of the economy is not static, but varies in response to alterations in the market structure of particular industry sectors. These alterations may reflect policy changes that are designed to promote or limit competition in a particular market. For example, advertising expenditure data by product sector in the UK in the 1980s shows how the deregulation of the UK financial services industry in the mid-1980s and the accompanying increase in competitive behaviour on the part of banks and building societies was reflected in an immediate and sharp increase in advertising expenditure by banks and building societies. In the 1990s, international deregulation of telecommunications brought about a great upsurge in advertising expenditure within this sector as new rivals emerged to compete with long-standing incumbents in the UK, across Europe and elsewhere.

The emergence of markets for successful new products or service innovations often has reverberations in the advertising sector. In the early part of the year 2000, a boom in the number of Internet start-ups created something of a bonanza for the advertising industry as many new 'dotcom' companies launched campaigns (using conventional media, such as billboards and television) as a means of raising awareness of themselves and their online businesses. A subsequent downturn in investor confidence in dotcom start-ups has since diminished some of this rich vein of new billings for advertising agencies. Even so, it is expected that expenditure on advertising by dot.com companies will, by itself, add around 3 per cent growth to total advertising in the USA and the UK in the year 2000 (Killgren, 2000: 7).

THE FIRM'S ADVERTISING DECISION

The decision each firm takes about how much of its resources to devote to advertising depends on what it believes this investment can achieve. What companies expect in return for their expenditure on advertising varies: whereas some simply want an effective marketing campaign, others believe that advertising agencies play a broader role in creating and managing their long-term brand strategies.

Systems of remuneration for advertising agencies have changed considerably in the UK over the last 10–15 years. Up until the late 1980s, most agencies expected to be paid a commission on 'gross billings' (i.e. the cost of all advertising space purchased on behalf of the client), usually at a rate of 15 per cent. US radio comedian Fred Allen coined the definition of an advertising agency as 85 per cent confusion and 15 per cent commission. The commission-based mode of payment not only encouraged agencies to concentrate their efforts on expensive media outlets but, more significantly, it ignored whether the advertising campaign supplied to the client was in any way effective or not. Nowadays, advertising agencies are generally paid on a flat fee basis and, in the UK, around one-third of their clients favour the concept of 'payment by results' (Hall, 2000b: 5). This approach raises a perplexing and long-standing question surrounding firms' expenditure on advertising – namely, how can the effectiveness of advertising be measured?

Many advertising clients put the 'payment by results' approach into operation by means of a sales-based model of compensation. In other words, the fee the advertising agency receives is calculated by reference to the impact of the advertising campaign on client sales. This seems fair, to the extent that the motivation behind advertising is simply to sustain or improve demand for the firm's products or services. However, some advertising clients regard this approach as too simplistic and prefer to measure their agencies' success by, for example, tracking studies that focus on perceptions of the firm and its brands.

The question of how to measure the effectiveness of advertising expenditure is important since, unless some idea can be gained about what return advertising will bring, firms will naturally find it very difficult to decide how much to spend on this activity. The two most common ways of researching the effectiveness of advertising involve either measuring the success of advertising in communicating its message, or direct tests of the effects of advertising on sales or profits. Both of these methods, however, have serious weaknesses.

In the case of testing people's ability to recall advertising messages, the obvious weakness is that this approach doesn't yield any reliable information about the impact on sales. How often does a clever visual or punch-line in an advertisement create a lasting impression but without successfully projecting the brand or having a discernible effect on demand? Studies that look more broadly at how advertising has affected perceptions of the firm and its brands suffer from the same problem – the impact of this expenditure on the firm's financial performance is not addressed. The capability for interactive advertising (e.g. on the Net) brings another way of measuring effectiveness: the number of responses an advertisement elicits can be counted. All in all, however, proof that advertising has engaged viewers' attention, has communicated a message successfully or has improved a brand or a corporate image is not the same as demonstrating an impact on profits.

So, for many advertisers, the second method – looking directly at sales – seems more useful, since the whole point of advertising is usually to boost sales. But there are also problems with this second method, to do with establishing any direct causal link between what a firm spends on advertising and what happens to sales. One immediate problem to be taken into account with direct testing is that advertising is not, itself, a homogeneous product. The effect on sales that a given expenditure on advertising will achieve depends, to a great extent, on the quality of the advertising campaign that has been purchased. Not all advertising agencies have equal talent. In the UK, for example, those advertising campaigns which seem to most clearly demonstrate a profitable return for clients are acknowledged each year by the Institute of Practitioners in Advertising (IPA) effectiveness awards competition. The way in which a firm's sales move or fail to move as a result of a campaign devised by one particular agency may not be a reliable indicator of how sales will typically or more generally respond to investment in advertising.

Another problem is that of time lags. It may take some time before advertising starts to have the desired impact on sales. Advertising might inspire an initial trial which might then result in positive recommendations to friends and, in turn, be followed by further purchases. Advertising may communicate its message successfully but at a time when the consumer is not yet in a position to make a purchase. So it may take some time before advertising has a visible impact on sales. It is often argued that consumers need to be exposed to a certain amount of advertising before they will respond but once they do respond, not much advertising is required to retain their loyalty. Advertising gradually builds up and then reinforces the positive perceptions of a product or brand or, in a sense, the 'goodwill' that is needed to ensure habitual purchasing of it. Indeed, the future earnings potential that investment in advertising is thought to have generated for a firm is sometimes recognized when famous brands are valued and accounted for as assets on a company balance sheet.

To deal with time lags, a regressive model is sometimes used to measure the effect of advertising. Advertising which has taken place in a previous period (say, the first quarter of 1999) is compared with current sales (in the first quarter of the following year). But a further and more insurmountable difficulty with measuring the effectiveness of a firm's expenditure on advertising is that of the behaviour of rivals. How do you disentangle the effect of advertising on demand for your product from the effect caused by whatever your rivals have been up to simultaneously in terms of advertising or not advertising their own wares, or implementing competitive price reductions, or instigating product changes or other special promotional efforts? It is virtually impossible for any firm in an oligopoly or a competitive market situation to isolate the impact of its own advertising investment from the impact on demand caused by the behaviour of its rivals.

So, the problems of measuring the effects of advertising are not simple and, in particular, it is very difficult to establish proof of some degree of causality, i.e. that x expenditure on advertising will have y given effect on sales (Carter, 1998: 6). How, then, do firms decide on their advertising budgets?

Economists who have considered this question – especially Cowling et al. (1975), Chiplin and Sturgess (1981) and Duncan (1981) – acknowledge that many firms simply use some kind of 'rule of thumb'. The decision taken about what level of resources to devote to advertising is often based on customary practice or what amounts to intuition rather than on any attempt to calculate expected returns. Sometimes advertising is regarded as discretionary rather than necessary expenditure and firms simply spend whatever they think they can afford at a given time. This approach is reflected in historic data, discussed above, which demonstrates the sensitivity of overall levels of advertising to company profits and to fluctuations in the economy at large. But the discretionary approach is often criticized on the basis of being too unscientific and unlikely to achieve great results.

Many firms set their advertising budget as a given proportion of sales or of assets. The pre-determined percentage of either previous or predicted sales is a particularly popular method – e.g. this year's advertising budget may be set at the rate of 10 per cent of last year's sales – and it offers various advantages. It is easy to calculate and it is quite manageable in financial terms, in the sense that the advertising budget will go up or down directly in accordance with the firm's fortunes.

But how does the firm decide what proportion of sales the advertising budget should represent? Analysis of historic sales and advertising figures reveals some very wide disparities between the proportions opted for by different firms. For example, according to statistics compiled by the Advertising Association (1996: 226), advertising accounted for just 5 per cent of what consumers spent on babycare products in 1994 but for a massive 44 per cent of consumer expenditure on double-glazing! Should the advertising budget be set at 5 per cent or 44 per cent of sales? Many firms examine what their competitors are spending and set their own advertising budget as a similar proportion of sales or assets. But there is no guarantee that the level set by competitors is optimal.

Some economic theorists have tried to provide a more scientific answer to this question. Dorfman and Steiner have suggested that, when it comes to deciding what proportion of sales income to devote to advertising, there are two things that firms should take into account: first, 'advertising elasticity' or how responsive sales are to changes in advertising expenditure and, second, 'price elasticity' or how responsive sales are to any change in price (Chiplin and Sturgess, 1981: 45). The reason why consumers' reactions to any price change should be taken into account in setting the advertising budget is because it would be inefficient to spend money on advertising if the same money invested in a price reduction would boost sales by a greater amount. If sales are more responsive to fluctuations in price than to changes in levels of advertising, this implies that a lower proportion of sales income should be devoted to advertising.

The Dorfman Steiner approach may have merit in theory but it is by no means easy to put into operation. Price elasticity refers to the responsiveness or sensitivity of demand to upward or downward movements in the price of a product. Likewise, the concept of advertising elasticity refers to the responsiveness of demand to changes in levels of advertising expenditure on that product. The problem is that it is virtually impossible to calculate advertising elasticity in 'real world' circumstances because of constant changes and the unpredictable behaviour of competitors.

ADVERTISING AND NEW MEDIA

The growth of new media such as the Internet and digital television has provided advertisers with a range of new communication channels through which they can address messages to their target audience groups. At first glance, the arrival of additional supplies of audience access seems to be a positive development, allowing for more specialist targeting and, potentially, lower advertising costs. However, the growing popularity of new media inevitably erodes mass audiences which, from the point of view of many advertisers, makes consumers more difficult to reach.

Just as newspaper proprietors were concerned about the development of advertising-supported broadcast media in the 1940s, so too the current generation of media players is anxious to assess the likely threat to commercial revenues posed by the development of the Internet, interactive television and other new multimedia products and services. The question they face is to what extent the rise of alternative avenues of communication with consumers may come at the expense of conventional advertising media and to what extent they may simply expand the overall advertising market. Will the growth of advertising in new media be incremental to or a substitute for traditional mass market advertising?

The capacity for interactivity facilitated by digital technology is a major concern for traditional advertising media. The Internet has already established itself, especially with younger audiences, as an important medium and interactive television is also well on its way towards gaining acceptance. Interactivity is, of course, driving the process of fragmentation of audiences into ever narrower niches and specialisms. More significantly, interactivity has the potential to provide advertisers with extensive information about the tastes, preferences and habits of particular sections of the audience. The facility for advertisers to get to know their target customer base – to learn about and speak to individual tastes amongst niche audiences – is a valuable advantage that conventional mass media cannot provide.

The Internet is now beginning to compete with traditional media for a share of some major advertisers' marketing budgets. According to the UK's Institute of Practitioners in Advertising, 'the number of companies allocating more than 5 per cent of their budgets to Internet marketing rose from 8 per cent to 14 per cent in the third quarter [of 2000]' (cited in Hall, 2000c: 6). The Internet is clearly better suited to some forms of advertising than others; for example, to provide classified rather than display advertisements, and to aim commercial messages at specific audience subgroups. Consequently, some conventional media – particularly those newspaper and magazine publishers who rely on targeted classified advertising – will find that their revenues are more threatened by the growth of the Internet than others.

New media such as the Internet, digital television and WAP[2] mobile phones offer users more choice and control over what sorts of entertainment or information services they wish to receive. On the one hand,

---

2. WAP or Wireless Application Protocol is a technology that allows consumers access to the Internet on their mobile phones.

personalized and interactive media consumption make it possible for advertisers to collect useful feedback and to foster closer and more effective two-way communication with relevant consumers. On the other, the cost of attracting the attention of large audiences via tailored one-to-one marketing is much more significant than via a campaign conveyed across conventional mass media. The price of advertising on the Internet, for example, currently running at around £30 per thousand 'page impressions' in the UK, is not far behind the price of a direct mail shot and is considerably more expensive than the cost per thousand (of around £10 and £3 respectively) for a 30-second commercial either on network television or radio (Oliver, 2000: 57). On a cost per capita basis, 'micro' marketing may prove expensive but, for some advertisers at least, it is also less wasteful than mass advertising in mainstream media.

Paradoxically perhaps, as audiences for traditional media have fragmented, the cost of reaching a mass of consumers has increased. The growing price and waning influence of advertising expenditure on main-stream television channels such as the four main 'over-the-air' networks in the US or the ITV network in the UK is a source of frustration for many advertisers, yet they are powerless to reverse the changes in lifestyle and in patterns of media consumption which make mass marketing an increasingly expensive exercise.

We live in an era in which famous brands are highly valued. So, even as audiences fragment across media catering to ever narrower sets of tastes, many advertisers continue to rely primarily on mainstream conventional media to create the mass consumer brands of the future. The greater ability of conventional media to reach mass audiences and to establish famous brands still remains a strong selling point. According to Hegarty, '[w]hat makes a brand is fame, and that comes from communicating with people *en masse*' (cited in Smith, 1998: 1). So, despite the fact that, in the UK as elsewhere, newspaper circulations are declining and television audiences are beginning to fragment, 'advertising prices are still being pushed up because the advertiser's need to find fame is more urgent than ever' (Hall, 2000a: 3).

So far at least, it seems that extra channels of communication and better opportunities for tailored marketing have stimulated incremental demand for advertising rather than diminishing appetites for commercial space in traditional media. For this reason, the arrival of new media is seen by many as a complement to rather than a substitute for conventional mass media. The effect of the Internet on advertising markets has been likened to 'adding a couple of lanes to the motorway – it just means that overall traffic levels get higher' (Gottlieb cited in Hall, 2000a: 3). 'Micro' marketing via new media is adding extra volumes of advertising activity rather than replacing mass marketing.

But new digital and interactive media are still in their infancy and until their full capability as marketing vehicles is understood, the future for advertiser-supported conventional media like television, radio and newspapers is uncertain. Traditional media are protected only so long as they remain the most convenient route to mass audiences. As new niche services continue to splinter audiences, the perceived level of substitutability between new and traditional advertising media will inevitably increase.

A fragmented audience is not the only problem facing advertisers. Some new media offer users the ability to bypass advertising altogether. For example, the emerging generation of digital video recorders, such as those offered by TiVo (manufactured by Royal Philips Electronics of the Netherlands) and ReplayTV (manufactured by Panasonic, a subsidiary of Matsushita of Japan), allow viewers to skip over the advertisements when they watch recorded television. Digital video recorders – also known as Personal Video Recorders (PVRs) – can record and store programmes by type in response to pre-selected choices made by the individual viewer and, at the same time, can edit out programme credits or other unwanted interruptions, including commercial breaks.

The ability for viewers to skip advertising has been heralded by some as 'the end of commercial television' (Lewis, 2000: 2). But opinions vary on how exactly PVRs will affect viewing habits. Video cassette recorders have always offered viewers the option of fast-forwarding to avoid commercial breaks in recorded material and this has not undermined advertiser-supported television broadcasting. PVRs, however, make it much easier to side-step advertising. The question is, to what extent will audiences continue to watch much of their television 'live', in spite of the greater convenience of recording thanks to PVRs?

According to Ave Butensky, President of US industry body the Television Advertising Bureau, (cited in Tomkins, 1999b: 19), viewers 'will figure out how to switch the television on and how to change the channel, but beyond that, they don't want to know. Basically, they're couch potatoes.' If, as Butensky suggests, most viewers ignore the arrival of the PVR and continue to flick passively between 'live' television channels, then audiences will not be able to skip over advertising breaks and commercial broadcasters have little to worry about. Many viewers will, however, undoubtedly be tempted by the possibility of their own customized pre-recorded programme schedule, and so PVRs will continue the process of erosion of audiences for conventional broadcast channels as well as making it progressively more difficult to entice audiences to watch television advertising.

four

TELEVISION BROADCASTING

Television is the largest component of the media industry in most developed economies. In the UK, television attracts some 28 per cent of total expenditure on advertising (Advertising Association, 2000: 4). In the US, it accounts for more than 20 per cent of all media revenues (Gasson, 1996: 114). The sector can be broadly subdivided into the activities of broadcasting and programme production, although some television companies are involved in both. The current chapter focuses on the economics of broadcasting while Chapter 5 examines the upstream activity of production or content-making.

This chapter examines alternative funding structures and mechanisms for television and considers market failures associated with broadcasting. The importance of economies of scale and scope are considered and the significance, for all broadcasters, of the concept of 'circles of profitability' is explained. Strategies of networking are analysed, drawing on suitable examples. The work of US economists on 'programme choice models' to explain competitive scheduling strategies is also reviewed.

After studying this chapter, you should be able to:

- Explain the economic characteristics associated with broadcasting
- Assess key positions in the debate over publicly funded broadcasting
- Analyse the advantages associated with strategies of networking
- Explain tendencies towards competitive duplication in scheduling strategies
- Analyse the importance of direct viewer payments as a mode of financing broadcasting

ECONOMIC CHARACTERISTICS OF TELEVISION BROADCASTING

Right from the outset, the characteristics of broadcasting made it a somewhat unusual activity in economic terms. Back in the 1920s, when the ability to transmit radio signals was first being experimented with, one of the big problems for aspiring broadcasters was to figure out a way of collecting money in return for this activity. There was no obvious means of identifying listeners and charging them directly for broadcast services. In a normal market, the price of a good and the quantity of it that will be supplied are determined by matching supply and demand. But in the early days of broadcasting, no method was available for viewers or listeners to register their demand patterns and preferences with suppliers. The absence of a mechanism to collect fees or to realize profits directly from audiences is termed a 'market failure' of broadcasting (Collins et al., 1988: 101; Blumler and Nossiter, 1991: 18).

Two different sorts of approach to overcoming this problem are discernible. In the UK, a form of public funding was organized. The government oversaw the establishment of a broadcaster which was a public corporation – the BBC – and was funded by a tax charged to all owners of broadcast receiving equipment in the UK: the BBC licence fee. In the US, the broadcasting industry had to develop on a commercial basis and so it turned to sponsorship. Its programmes were paid for by companies such as Procter & Gamble, who were allowed to introduce these programmes with commercial messages about their products.

Helped along by advertising and, more recently, by viewer subscriptions, the commercial television industry has grown steadily and flourished over the last few decades, not only in the USA but also in most other countries. However, the potential for market failure is still present because of the exceptional nature of broadcast output. That output takes two different forms. Like the rest of the media, television broadcasting generally takes place in what is referred to as a 'dual-product' market (Picard, 1989: 17). The first product of a television broadcaster is its programme service – i.e. the elements of televisual input (programmes, advertisements, continuity, etc.) arranged into a schedule or service which viewers or audiences may 'consume' upon receipt – and it is this type of output that is imbued with characteristics which, in economic terms, are quite unusual.

The television broadcaster's other product is, of course, its audiences, i.e. the viewers who tune in to watch its programme service. Access to audiences may be priced and sold to advertisers. The way in which commercial airtime is sold to advertisers varies from one territory to another and, sometimes, between different broadcasters. Generally speaking, it is traded according to the size of the audience it reaches but sometimes it may be sold on a 'flat rate' basis – i.e. at a fixed price per (say, 30-second) advertising spot. When advertising is sold according to the size of the audience, this typically involves looking at ratings predictions for the broadcaster's programme schedule and then booking sufficient slots to reach an audience of a given size and demographic profile. So the audience ratings actually achieved by the broadcaster will play a vital role in determining its income. A television company with falling ratings may find that it has pre-sold access to a larger audience than it is able to deliver. Consequently, it will be forced to cut back on advertising sales in subsequent periods in order to complete its sales contracts with advertisers. Conversely, a television company whose ratings are rising faster than anticipated will complete its sales contracts early and then have additional advertising space left over to sell (Gasson, 1996: 147–8).

The broadcaster's first form of output – i.e. the programme service by which audiences are attracted – has what are called 'public-good' attributes (Owen and Wildman, 1992: 23–4). As discussed earlier, a public good is one which, once produced, can be consumed by everyone in society (Lipsey and Chrystal, 1995: 896). Television has the qualities of a public good because the way it is consumed by any individual viewer does not reduce its supply for everyone else. The essential quality from which the consumer value of a television broadcast derives is not physical. Instead, it is in the meanings or messages conveyed. These are immaterial and do not get used up in the act of consumption (Collins et al., 1988: 6; Blumler and Nossiter, 1991: 10–11).

The marginal cost of transmitting to an extra television viewer is usually zero (Pratten, 1970: 16), although this depends on the distribution system concerned. With terrestrial television transmitted over the airwaves, the marginal cost is usually zero, unless a new transmitter has to be built to reach that extra viewer. With cable television, the connection cost has to be included. For pay-television services, some marginal subscriber management costs will arise, but these are relatively modest. Generally speaking, it costs virtually nothing to supply a television broadcast service to an extra customer, so there are great economies of scale involved as the audience grows. Conversely, there are no savings for television broadcasters when audiences are squeezed.

These characteristics have significant implications for the finances of any new television channel. When a new channel is launched, the only way to build up an audience is to invest in programming. However, programming is expensive. At the same time, the audience for a new channel will be low, which implies that little or no revenue can be earned in the early stages. To avoid getting into a vicious circle of low programme budgets and deteriorating audiences – see Figure 4.1 – a new channel must sustain its investment in programme quality regardless of the fact that audiences and revenues will not, initially, cover these costs.

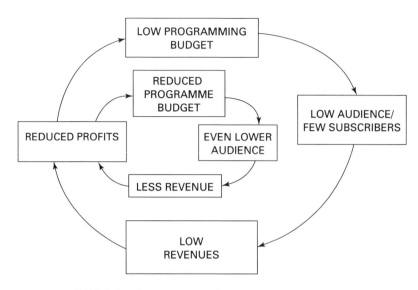

FIGURE 4.1   Vicious circles of profitability in broadcasting

In most industries, suppliers are able to tailor output levels and (importantly) costs in response to demand. If demand slackens, suppliers can cushion themselves to some extent by cutting back on, say, raw materials. But broadcasting doesn't work like that. The cost of providing a given programme service is relatively fixed, regardless of how many, if any, viewers tune in. So, in order to cover its fixed costs, every commercial broadcaster needs to attract a certain minimum number of viewers or subscribers. Inevitably, operating losses will be experienced when viewership falls short of this level. However, if a vicious downward spiral is to be avoided, weak audience figures must not be allowed to impinge on programming budgets.

It is only by sustaining its investment in programming that a broadcaster can hope to break into a 'virtuous' circle of improving audiences and higher programme budgets (see Figure 4.2). It may take four or five years or even longer before a new channel has built up its revenue base to the point where it begins to break even (Brown, 1999: 14). But once a sufficient number of viewers or subscribers have been attracted to cover fixed operating costs, the broadcaster can start to make considerable profits. Because the marginal costs of serving extra viewers are low, a very high proportion of any additional revenues at this stage will flow through into profits. And as it becomes more profitable, the broadcaster may decide to increase its investment in content so as to underpin the strength and popularity of its programme service.

In the UK, BSkyB – the dominant satellite broadcaster – provides a good example of a television company that has broken into a virtuous circle

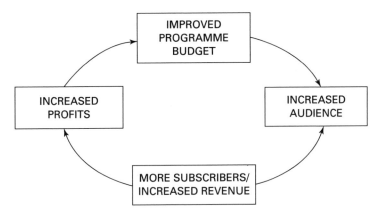

FIGURE 4.2   Virtuous circles of profitability in broadcasting

of profitability. In the early 1990s, BSkyB's shareholders endured considerable losses because the revenues which could be earned from the available audience for satellite television in the UK were not sufficient to match BSkyB's investment in programming. Because weak audience figures were not allowed to impinge on programme budgets, BSkyB managed to avoid a spiral of decline. The company acknowledges that the strategy of pumping money into programming, and of creating a virtuous circle, has been the key to its commercial success: 'BSkyB's clear strategy of using the resources which its subscribers provide to invest in quality and diverse programming drives subscription growth, which then provides further resources for programming investment' (BSkyB, 1996: 28). Starting in 2001, the company is expected to make the transition from heavy investment in building market share to an era of high profitability, but it has taken more than a decade to arrive at this point (Harding, 2001b: 26).

The per-viewer costs of providing a television programme service reduce sharply as audiences increase and so television broadcasting very clearly lends itself to economies of scale. Economies of scope are another feature of the industry – i.e. savings that arise as the firm diversifies its output. Economies of scope will be present if there are some shared overheads, or other efficiency gains available that make it more cost-effective for two or more related products to be supplied jointly under common ownership, rather than by separate firms (Moschandreas, 1994: 155). For example, economies of scope will arise in television broadcasting whenever savings can be made by exploiting the same content or intellectual property across more than one form of output (i.e. more than one programme or more than one programme service).

The term 'economies of scope' is also used to refer to the practice within broadcasting of subsidization of one type of programming by another.

When used in that way, economies of scope can be seen as a way of counteracting some of the risks inherent in the business of broadcasting (Collins et al., 1988: 11; Blumler and Nossiter, 1991: 12–13). The broadcaster offers a whole range of products (elements of programming), with some parts of the schedule designed to appeal to some parts of the audience and others to a different set of individuals. Consumers will tune in so long as a high enough proportion is to their taste. This control over a range of products greatly increases the broadcaster's chances of making a hit with consumer taste. The revenue (or audience value) from a hit compensates the broadcaster for the cost of producing the whole schedule or 'portfolio' of programmes. In other words, the strength of individual programmes in a schedule is used to spread risk and equalize costs across a range of total output designed to generate the greatest possible audience value or appeal.

MARKET FAILURES IN BROADCASTING

Broadcasting is beset by a number of market failures, many of which stem from the public-good characteristics of broadcast output discussed above. Free markets generally work well to allocate normal or 'private' goods but, when it comes to public goods, they do not always function properly. The term 'market failure' tends to be used in two different ways. In one sense it refers to any failure by the market system – the unbridled forces of demand and supply – to allocate resources efficiently. In another sense, it may refer to the failure of the market to advance socially desirable goals other than efficiency, such as preserving democracy and social cohesion.

Looking first at efficiency problems, the most striking case of market failure in broadcasting is that radio and television would not, in the first place, have been produced at all by private profit-seeking firms were they reliant on the conventional mechanism of market funding – i.e. direct payments from consumers. The market system could not have compelled payment for broadcasting because there was no way to identify those who were receiving it and there was no way to prevent anyone who refused to pay for broadcasting from being able to receive it anyway.

Public goods often have the characteristic of being **non-excludable**. This refers to the difficulty of excluding those who don't want to pay for something. For example, a national defence establishment protects everybody in a country, whether they want it or not and whether they are prepared to pay for it or not. Terrestrial broadcasting services are usually available to everyone, whether individual viewers are willing to pay for them or not. With any good or service that is non-excludable and where customers do not have exclusive rights to consume the good in question, it is difficult to make 'free riders' pay for it (Griffiths and Wall, 1999: 174). So, the free market is unlikely to provide these sorts of goods efficiently.

Public goods also have the characteristic of being **non-exhaustible**. This refers to the fact that there are zero marginal costs involved in supplying the service to one additional viewer. Because of this, and because extra 'consumption' of television output does not reduce the supply available to other viewers, this implies that no one should be preventing from receiving any broadcast service. 'Restricting the viewing of programmes that, once produced, could be made available to everyone at no extra cost, leads to inefficiency and welfare losses' (Davies, 1999: 203). On the other hand, if no one can be excluded from receiving broadcast services, then payment for broadcasting cannot be compelled and the economic incentive to supply some forms of output will be removed.

Another cause of failure in broadcasting markets relates to the problem of **asymmetric information**. What consumers are offered by broadcasters is the opportunity for new knowledge or a new entertainment experience. But viewers cannot know in advance whether they will value this experience or not and how much it is worth to them. It is only by 'consuming' what is on offer that viewers will get a sense of its worth but, once they have watched a television show, there is no longer any incentive to pay for it. In short, '[p]eople do not know what they are "buying" until they have experienced it, yet once they have experienced it they no longer need to buy it!' (Graham and Davies, 1997: 19).

An important source of market failure stems from what are referred to as **externalities** or external effects. Externalities are costs or, in some cases, benefits imposed on third-parties. They arise when the private costs to a firm of engaging in a certain activity are out of line with its social costs. Pollution provides a good example of a negative externality. An individual firm may neglect the external effects of its actions when it discharges hazardous waste into rivers because its own profits are not affected by this activity. Broadcasting can have adverse external effects. The provision of some sorts of content may engender a wider cost to society, for example by increasing levels of violence or fear of violence in society. The fact that these costs are not borne by the broadcaster results in market failure because broadcasters may devote more resources to providing television output with negative external effects than is socially optimal.

So, when it comes to broadcasting, there are several ways in which a completely unregulated market might fail to allocate resources efficiently. However, any notion that the market *should* act as the main determinant of how resources are allocated depends, in the first instance, on the belief that individuals and households are the best judges of their own interests. Here opinions differ. Some favour a paternalistic approach towards broadcasting.

A **merit good** (or service) is one where the Government takes the view that more of it should be produced than people would choose to consume, if left to their own devices. Several different motives may be implied when something is treated as a merit good. It may be 'because it confers positive externalities, or because the Government feels people are not the best judges of their own interests, or because it feels that production of the good contributes to the maintenance of certain social values that cannot be expressed in market terms' (Lipsey and Chrystal, 1995: 406).

Broadcasting seems to fit into all of these categories. It can confer positive externalities. There are some forms of content that are collectively desirable and that everyone benefits from (e.g. documentaries, educational and cultural programmes) but which viewers, on an individual basis, might not tune into or be prepared to pay for. Just as with education or training, consumers tend to buy less 'good' programming than is in their own long-term interests. So, under free market circumstances, programming that is intrinsically 'good' will be under-supplied. Davies suggests that '[i]f all television is provided via the free market, there is a danger that consumers will under-invest in their own tastes, experience and capacity to comprehend because it is only in retrospect that the benefits of such investment become apparent' (1999: 203).

PUBLICLY FUNDED BROADCASTING

The most commonly used policy tools to address market failures in broadcasting are regulation and public ownership. Licensing and **regulation** of commercial television broadcasting are carried out in the UK by the Independent Television Commission (ITC). The regulatory authority for broadcasting in the US is the Federal Communications Commission (FCC). Regulation (both structural and content-related) is a common feature of television markets and, typically, it involves rules that encourage privately owned broadcasters to deviate from profit-maximizing strategies where necessary to meet public requirements concerning quality of output. Broadcasting has always been one of the most heavily regulated sectors of the economy and regulation is one of the key factors influencing the financial performance and prospects for commercial television companies (Gasson, 1996: 8–9).

A second and, arguably, more effective way of counteracting market failures is through **public ownership** of broadcasting. The public-good characteristics of broadcasting – the fact that it is non-excludable and non-exhaustible – imply that it would best be supplied by the public sector at zero price, using public funds to finance provision. Another advantage of public as opposed to private ownership is that, rather than worrying about shareholders, managers can devote themselves exclusively to 'public service' broadcasting. Indeed, most countries have established some sort of publicly funded and state-owned broadcasting entity to provide public service broadcasting (PSB).

However, the use of public funds to finance broadcasting is controversial. One of the main points of concern is that support from public funding denies consumer sovereignty. Some people believe that, in principle, the provision of any service – including broadcasting – is best left to market forces. This begs the question of whether, as suggested above, the peculiarities of broadcasting are such that the market system would fail to provide people with the broadcasting services they want.

Until recently, the main source of market funding for broadcasting was advertising. Advertising is a faulty funding mechanism in that it creates an incentive for the broadcaster to maximize not overall viewer welfare but the supply of whatever mix of programming yields the audiences that advertisers particularly want to reach. Reliance on advertising creates a focus on attaining large audience volumes, while patterns of intensity of viewer demand for different sorts of output may be ignored.

But advertising is no longer the only funding option. Because of advances in encryption technology, direct payments from viewers have come to represent an increasingly important revenue stream for commercial broadcasters. So a well-functioning market in television broadcasting now seems feasible. The possibility of direct viewer payments implies that demand and supply for public service content could also be matched up directly, thus removing the need for a 'distorted' funding mechanism or public funds.

In the UK, the BBC's public service output is funded through a compulsory licence fee imposed on all homes where a television set is owned (irrespective of whether or not BBC services are watched). Peacock (1996), Graham et al. (1999) and others have focused attention on the question of whether or not, in an increasingly competitive broadcasting market, this form of public funding has now become outdated. Positions are divided. Arguments against the licence fee highlight the fact that we no longer suffer from spectrum scarcity, that audiences are fragmenting and that the technology necessary to allow viewers to make payments directly for whatever broadcasting services they want has arrived. Since it is unfair to make everyone pay for services they may not want to watch, a voluntary payment would be preferable to a compulsory universal tax as a means of supporting public service broadcasting. An old-fashioned paternalistic

PSB system is undesirable when a 'free market' in television broadcasting is now entirely feasible and would give viewers exactly what they want.

Others, however, take the view that '[a]lthough private markets in broadcasting may be good in some areas, on their own they will generally fail to produce the overall quality of broadcasting that consumers individually or collectively would desire' (Porter, 1999: 36). As discussed earlier, some forms of PSB content which are desirable and which everybody benefits from, but which viewers do not always want to tune in to or pay for on an individual basis, will be under-supplied in a free market. Conversely, television output which creates negative externalities may be over-supplied. So, even with direct viewer payments, market failures persist. The problem remains that in charging for broadcast services, some viewers will be excluded whose enjoyment would exceed the marginal cost of providing the service.

An unregulated free market for broadcasting will result in some deficiencies. But the use of public funds to finance broadcasting also raises problems. Amongst those who agree that the provision of PSB is desirable and that a free market will not adequately supply this, opinions are divided about which methods of public finance ought to be used. Some regard the compulsory licence fee favoured in the UK as inherently unfair. Peacock (1996) accepts that there are arguments for continuing with the fee but questions whether the proceeds should be put out to competitive tender (thus allowing other broadcasters to bid for the opportunity to supply UK viewers and listeners with PSB) rather than simply awarded to the BBC.

In Australia, public service broadcasting output is paid for through a public grant. State funding, however, raises questions about how the independence of public broadcasters can be preserved. In Greece, PSB is partly paid for through a levy imposed on consumers' electricity bills. As with a compulsory licence fee, however, the incidence and level of charges imposed for PSB bear no relation to patterns of usage or demand and so this may be considered an unfair system. Across Europe, many public service broadcasters are funded partly by advertising and partly by public finances. But reliance on advertising creates an incentive for PSBs to compete with private broadcasters for audience ratings and this practice has resulted in complaints to DG IV (the European Commission's competition authority) from commercial television rivals about unfair competition. Clearly, then, there is no easy answer to the question of which funding mechanism for PSB is most desirable.

THE VERTICAL SUPPLY CHAIN FOR TELEVISION

The television industry involves several key stages. First, there is **production** of television programmes, which is usually carried out by programme-makers. Television programme production firms draw together raw materials such as scripts and actors or other talent and convert these into finished products ready for transmission to viewers. Programmes (or, more specifically, the transmission rights for given programmes) are then sold to service **packagers** who assemble television schedules. Then the television service, as a package, is distributed onwards to viewers by **broadcasters**. Some service packagers are broadcasters themselves, but others are separate intermediaries, such as the major US networks ABC, NBC, CBS and Fox.

The distribution phase for broadcast television can sometimes be broken into more than one stage (see Figure 4.3). For example, with pay television, **distribution** (carried out by broadcasters) may be regarded as a separate function from managing and administering the consumer interface. Management of the interface with subscribers or management of whatever conditional access system (the system of encryption needed to charge viewers) is used may sometimes be carried out by entities other than the channel distributor.

Some television companies are involved in several or all of the major stages along the vertical supply chain. In the UK, for example, the ITV network is the most popular commercial television channel and most of its participant companies are vertically integrated in the sense that they make programmes as well as being broadcasters. Others are involved in only one stage. Channel Four, for example, another UK television broadcaster, offers a full and varied schedule but does not make any programmes itself. Instead it acquires one-off transmission rights or else commissions the production of new programmes for its schedule from separate or 'independent' television production companies.

In the US, there has been an interesting history of Government intervention in the vertical supply chain for television through what were called the Financial Interest and Syndication or 'Finsyn' rules (Owen and Wildman, 1992: 202). These are restrictions which, from 1970 until 1995, limited the extent of vertical integration between what were then the three major television broadcast networks (ABC, CBS and NBC) and content-

FIGURE 4.3   Vertical supply chain for television

makers mostly based in Hollywood (Litman, 1998: 142). The Finsyn rules limited the extent to which the networks were allowed to share in any profits from secondary sales of the programmes they aired, thus effectively preventing these three large corporations from getting involved in the television production business.

A similar kind of regulatory intervention was introduced more recently in the UK. Following on from the recommendations of the 1986 Peacock Report (on broadcasting finance), the 1990 Broadcasting Act introduced a compulsory 25 per cent access quota for independent producers at ITV and the BBC. The main television broadcasters in the UK have been required, since 1990, to purchase around a quarter of their programming output from television production companies that are 'independent' – i.e. not owned by themselves or any other broadcaster.

Interventions of this sort are intended to prevent powerful vertically integrated broadcasting entities from dominating the entire supply chain for television. Policy-makers have sought to increase competition within programme-making and to provide opportunities for the content production sector to develop separately from the broadcasting sector. However, as levels of competition in the distribution phase for television have escalated, and as content-producers themselves have begun to embark on strategies of vertical expansion, it is clear that the ease with which broadcasters have dominated the television industry has diminished. Even so, broadcasting networks are still very often the market leaders within commercial television and radio.

NETWORKS

The economic logic behind strategies of networking is highly compelling. A network is an arrangement whereby a number of local or regional television or radio stations are linked together for the purposes of creating and exploiting mutual economic benefits (Owen and Wildman, 1992: 206). The most important benefit created is usually economies of scale in programming. A network of broadcasters in different localities can share more or less exactly the same schedule of programmes. This reduces the per-viewer costs of providing the television service for each station in the network. So networks are a way of enlarging the audience for a single television service.

The UK provides the example of the ITV network. With a peak-time viewing share of 37 per cent (Competition Commission, 2000: 89), ITV is by far the most popular commercial channel in Britain and it comprises a network of 14 regional licences covering the whole of the UK. Ownership of these licences has been consolidating since the early 1990s and most are now controlled by just three firms: Granada Media, Carlton Communications and the Scottish Media Group. The ITV network shares programmes through a system where each of the 14 licencees contributes a payment into a collective budget for the ITV schedule of programmes and, in return, receives the right to broadcast that schedule (interspersed with some dedicated local output) in their own region. Each licencee makes money by selling advertising slots in and around transmissions of the ITV network schedule in its own regions.

Payments into the collective programme budget vary according to the respective revenue shares of participants in the network. So, ITV's arrangements for sharing costs involve some cross-subsidization of smaller regional licencees by larger ones. Even so, each participant – whether large or small – benefits greatly from being able to transmit a much more expensive schedule of programmes than it could afford if it were trying to operate independently.

In the USA, the main television networks – ABC, NBC, CBS and Fox – carry out two key functions (Owen and Wildman, 1992: 153; Litman, 1998: 131). Not only do they facilitate sharing the costs of programming in the same way as the ITV network, but the US networks also club together to sell advertising. Advertisers who want national coverage in the US can purchase it all in one go from the networks. This reduces transaction costs for national advertisers and increases demand for the airtime of local broadcasters participating in a network.

The USA networks rely on a chain of local television stations or 'affiliates' – around 200 each – to provide national audiences for their programmes. Each of the networks owns a few of its own affiliates but many are independently owned. What the local affiliates get from the network is a ready-made package for transmission (comprising a fairly comprehensive schedule of programmes together with advertisements) plus 'compensation' or a payment for accepting it (the amount of which varies from station to station). Network affiliates gain some $600 million annually in return for carrying prime-time programmes supplied by the networks and they are allowed opportunities to sell some commercial airtime of their own to both national and local advertisers. This facilitates high profit margins for most local affiliates (Gapper, 1998: 22).

By contrast, the US networks have experienced a squeeze on profits in recent years as more competition in the packaging phase from newcomers such as Fox has increased the bargaining power of affiliates (1998: 22). The incentive for networks to expand vertically and take on more self-owned local stations is greater than ever but the extent to which they are permitted to do so is curtailed by the 1996 Telecommunications Act which limits to 35 per cent the total share of the US television audience that any single company can reach. The networks gained a concession when, in 1999, the rules were partially relaxed to allow a single company to own two stations in the same local market for the first time (Parkes, 1999: 19). Owning two stations in the same market enables the broadcaster to 'stream' its output so as to achieve a more valuable demographic profile – i.e. to simultaneously transmit different programmes targeted at different audience segments – and it also facilitates cost savings on staff, studios, etc. (Grimes, 2000: 27). The networks have responded quickly to exploit this liberalizing measure: Fox, for example, has established duopolies both in New York and Los Angeles – the two top television markets in the USA.

Although established television networks everywhere are faced with increasing competition from new terrestrial, cable, satellite and digital broadcasting rivals, the level of advertising revenue they can attract generally tends to decline at a slower pace than their audience share. This is true both of the US networks and of the ITV network in the UK (Gasson, 1996: 148–50). In an increasingly fragmented market, the ability to make an immediate impact on mass audiences commands a special value. So advertisers are usually prepared to pay a premium on top of the usual cost per thousand rate for airtime that gives them access to mass audiences. Audiences during prime time and in the slots around particularly popular programmes typically sell at a higher CPT than in other periods. Likewise, audiences for the most popular channels sell at a premium. The collective audience share for the three major US networks – NBC, CBS and ABC – may well have declined by a third to around 42 per cent over the course of the 1990s (Parkes, 1999: 19), but these channels still offer the only means of reaching a genuinely mass television audience in the USA.

The advantages of scale that accrue to major networks can act as a barrier to entry in broadcasting. The economies of scale in programming available to established networks with large audiences make it very difficult for new entrants to break into the market. A new broadcaster usually has a long way to go before its audience reach will be sufficient to start earning the revenues needed to pay for a programme service that is directly competitive with existing networks (see Figure 4.2, p. 63). In the UK, for example, ITV's annual programme budget is around £850 million, as compared with £120 million for terrestrial newcomer Channel 5 and less than £20 million for some new pay-television channels (Competition Commission, 2000: 228).

When the strength of the networks is reinforced by strategies of vertical integration, the barriers to entry are even more difficult to overcome. According to the Chairman of USA Networks, Barry Diller, backward vertical integration has become an essential strategy for broadcast networks in order to control inflation in content costs: 'I don't think there is any way the [business] model can work unless you are making programming and owning it through every part of the value chain you can find' (cited in Gapper, 1998: 22). This view is evidently shared by the major US networks, including ABC which merged with Disney in 1995. Fox took the concept of vertical expansion a stage further when its parent company, News Corporation, acquired the Los Angeles Dodgers baseball team in the late 1990s. A similar strategy was attempted when Murdoch-owned satellite broadcaster BSkyB tried to take over Manchester United Football Club but was prevented from doing so by UK competition authorities in 1999. These moves reflect the increasing importance of ownership of rights to sports and other attractive programming in competition between broadcast networks.

In terms of viewer welfare, the prevalence of broadcasting networks can be criticized for contributing to uniformity of television output across different regions. On the other hand, since networks facilitate enormous economies of scale, it can be argued that the cost-savings they create make it possible for local and regional audiences to have more expensive and better programme services than could be afforded if local or regional broadcasters were stand-alone operations. The cost-savings enjoyed on prime-time programming by local stations that are part of a wider network should leave more resources available to invest in any parts of the schedule not supplied by the network – e.g. dedicated regional programming.

COMPETITIVE SCHEDULING STRATEGIES

It is often assumed that one of the benefits of competition is that it widens the range and quality of goods made available to consumers, while monopoly is to be avoided because it leads to uniformity of output. Broadcasting, however, provides an interesting counter-example. Competition between a few broadcasters can encourage copycat programming strategies and lead to more uniformity of output than would occur in a monopoly.

Lipsey offers the example of a radio audience comprising two groups: 80 per cent who prefer pop music and 20 per cent who want to hear classical music (1989: 394). It is assumed that each individual radio station will want to maximize its own audience. So, if there is only one station then it will obviously offer pop rather than classical music. A second competing station would also offer pop music, since half of the large audience for pop music is better than the whole minority audience for classical music. Likewise, a third station will offer a similar pop music-based service in order to vie for one-third of the 80 per cent audience segment. It is only when five stations are present that it will become more profitable to switch strategies and offer a classical music service. However (and perhaps ironically), if the market was served by a monopolist with two stations rather than by several competing station owners, the monopolist would find that the best way to maximize its total listening audience would be to adopt a strategy of market segmentation and devote one station to pop music and the other to classical music.

The phenomenon of **competitive duplication** in programming is easily understood by anyone familiar with the television services offered to US audiences. Programme schedules and formats on the major US networks tend to look incredibly similar and, at any given moment, each of the networks is likely to be offering a programme in exactly the same strand. In order to understand this behaviour, US economists have developed what are called **programme choice models**. The Beebe model, which typifies these, highlights various factors that determine the range of programmes offered including the structure of viewer preferences among different programme types, the number of television channels in existence, the competitive structure of the markets they operate in and the means of support for their services (Owen and Wildman, 1992: 99).

Programme choice models suggest that if most viewers want the same types of programme and television is supported by advertising payments, then competing broadcasters are likely to offer highly similar programmes targeted at this mass audience. The number of programmes designed to satisfy majority tastes will be excessive because competing channels will find it more profitable to carve up the majority-taste audience (by offering close substitutes) than to cater for minority tastes by alienating the majority. The greater the degree of conformity in audience tastes, the greater the tendency towards competitive duplication. In an unregulated market, the interests of minorities will be served only if the number of channels is large enough to exhaust the profits in competitive duplication, making minority-taste programming as profitable as majority-taste programming at the margin (assuming that minority-taste audiences are large enough to cover programme costs).

Other approaches to demonstrating the tendency towards competitive duplication in programming include that of Dunnett (1993: 57) who refers to the copycat tendency in programme scheduling as 'the law of central tendency'. If the tastes of viewers are examined, then, according to Dunnett, broadcasters will find that the centre, represented by game shows and situation comedies, can support many suppliers before it becomes worthwhile to target the fringes. Another kind of model – the Hotelling model of competitive behaviour – has also been used to illustrate the dangers to programme diversity in a deregulated market (Hughes and Vines, 1989: 44). The Hotelling model uses the analogy of two ice-cream sellers on a straight beach with walls at either end and holidaymakers spread evenly along the whole length of the beach. Assuming that they don't compete with each other on price, then the most competitive solution for both ice-cream sellers will be to locate side by side in the middle of the beach. If either seller were to move to the right or the left, then he or she would lose market share to the other. Likewise, for two television broadcasters that do not compete on price, the best option for both is to offer virtually identical mainstream programme services.

These models provide quite a useful way for considering competitive programming strategies in an unregulated advertiser-supported broadcasting environment with few channels. However, they begin to fail when direct charges to the viewer, multiple sellers and competition based on price are introduced. The television industry is now a much more pluralistic and complex environment than it was a couple of decades ago. Because of the arrival of new technologies, avenues for delivery of commercial television have expanded dramatically. Penetration rates for multichannel television still vary considerably but, in most developed economies, an array of 'new' channels are now operating in competition with traditional terrestrial broadcasters. In addition, commercial television companies now have the ability to charge viewers directly in return for programme services instead of relying solely on advertising. These developments have radically altered the structure of television broadcasting markets and the implications for the competitive behaviour of market participants are far-reaching.

IMPACT OF NEW DISTRIBUTION TECHNOLOGIES

Technology is a major force affecting the economics of the media and especially the television industry. Two important technological changes affecting distribution of television signals have taken place in recent years. First, the arrival of cable, satellite and, more recently, digital compression techniques have facilitated a continuous expansion in the way in which television can be distributed to viewers. This expansion has impacted on the industry's competitive market structure. Monopoly and duopoly have given way to increasingly competitive markets as the traditional barrier to market entry of spectrum scarcity has been eroded. In the longer term, broadcasting over the Internet, or 'webcasting', holds out the possibility of another exponential increase in the number of television channels.

The expansion in delivery methods for television has meant that the emphasis of scarcity in broadcasting has gradually shifted away from the means of distribution (from having a television channel) and onto content production (to having competitive programming to fill these new channels). In a multichannel environment, success as a broadcaster depends on securing ongoing access to the rights for distinctive and attractive programming. Consequently, the bargaining power of television rights owners (such as the Premier League which controls football rights in the UK) has increased. At the same time, strategies of upstream vertical integration have become more prevalent, where permitted, because of the urgent need for programme formats and software rights.

More outlets for television and more intense competition between broadcasters have inevitably resulted in a migration of viewers away from mainstream channels. In the USA, where multichannel television has been around for some years, the share of prime-time viewing accounted for by the three major US networks fell from around 90 per cent in 1980 to 60 per cent in 1990 to around 40 per cent in 2000. Across Europe, the spread of multichannel television has arrived later and progressed more slowly. Even so, in the UK the audience share accounted for by the BBC's two channels plus ITV fell from around 100 per cent in 1980 to less than 70 per cent in 2000.

As far as advertisers are concerned, increased competition amongst broadcasters and fragmentation of mass audiences are something of a mixed blessing. On the positive side, some of the new television channels clearly offer good opportunities for tailored marketing and, in theory, more competition ought to exert downward pressure on airtime prices. In the UK, for example, the CPT advertising rate for adults on pay-television channels averaged some £5.09 in 2000 – a discount of 29 per cent when compared with the adult CPT rate on ITV (Competition Commission, 2000: 99–101). On the negative side, the erosion of ratings for mainstream channels means that it is gradually becoming more difficult and, in reality, more expensive to reach mass audiences. In the UK, ITV's CPT rate for adults increased by 33 per cent from 1995 to 1999, even though ITV's share of total UK viewing was in decline during this period (ibid.). The paradox of increased competition leading to higher advertising costs is explained by the fact that, as audiences shrink, advertisers are obliged to buy ever-increasing amounts of airtime (at inflated prices on mainstream channels) to reach the required number of viewers.

The second important technological development is that advances in encryption and decoding technologies have facilitated the growth of a new source of funding for television – namely, direct payments from viewers. Subscription television was first introduced in the USA in the 1970s and its popularity grew in the UK and elsewhere in Europe throughout the 1990s. Subscriptions and other direct viewer payments now represent a significant revenue stream for broadcasting. For example, BSkyB's sub-scription revenue of some £1 billion per year compares with a total expenditure on television advertising in the UK of some £4 billion per annum (Advertising Association, 2000: 14). So viewer payments have clearly expanded the resources available for producing and acquiring television content, thus supporting many new television channels.

Before the arrival of direct viewer payments, there often existed for television what is known as a **consumer surplus**. A consumer surplus refers to the difference between what the consumer would be willing to pay for a product or service and what they actually have to pay in terms of the going market price (Griffiths and Wall, 1999: 93). The existence of a consumer surplus in broadcasting means that some or most viewers would have been prepared to pay more for certain programmes than was required. For example, sports enthusiasts may have been prepared to pay a high price to watch football matches, but the technology of broadcasting did not allow this. Direct payments have enabled broadcasters to tap into this consumer surplus and take advantage of a high intensity of preference for particular types of programming. Using this surplus, subscription income has made it feasible to supply some narrower audience segments, thus extending the diversity of television content.

The direct charge is an important source of support for niche, specialist and 'premium' programme content. BSkyB and other subscription-funded broadcasters have been able to use direct viewer payments to fund more thematic channels (children's programming, music, etc.) and to acquire exclusive rights to 'must see' programming (special events, films, etc.). So, direct payments have facilitated a move towards what is sometimes called **narrowcasting** as opposed to broadcasting. The programming strategies deployed by pay-television operators involve specialization and differentiation between different audience segments according to tastes and interests, in much the same way as takes place in consumer magazine publishing.

The growth of pay television has led to bidding wars for attractive content and to high inflation in the costs of certain programmes. Sport, for example, has been identified as a useful bait to entice large and valuable segments of the viewing public to migrate towards whatever channels it is distributed on. Rupert Murdoch famously described sports and films as the 'battering rams' of pay television. In the UK, subscription income has enabled satellite broadcaster BSkyB to outbid terrestrial rivals for access to the sorts of films and key sporting events which are most appealing to viewers. BSkyB is able to pass the cost of these expensive programme rights directly onto the viewer, either in the form of high subscriptions or in a pay-per-view charge. Advertiser-supported broadcasters simply cannot do this. So the growth of subscription funding is inevitably shifting not only audiences but also economic power away from advertising-funded channels to pay-television operators.

To the extent that the range and quality of programming have expanded since the arrival of viewer payments, there is a welfare gain for consumers – at least, for those who can afford monthly subscriptions for additional television choices. On the other hand, inflation in programming costs has affected the output of all broadcasters, especially those whose funding structures make it impossible to recoup on expenditure in premium programming areas. For example, as far as sports coverage is concerned, the advent of direct payments and the migration of top sporting events away from mass audiences and to a minority of paying viewers has created something of a 'two-tier' economy amongst television sports fans (Booth and Doyle, 1997: 278).

The zero-cost public-good attributes of broadcast output give rise to another drawback for direct viewer payments. In essence, the economic conditions for efficient allocation of a public good require that it should be given away for free (Owen and Wildman, 1992: 23). This is because whatever price is charged for pay television will exclude viewers to an extent not justified by the marginal costs that would be involved in allowing them to have the service.

All methods of broadcasting finance seem to involve deficiencies, but broadcasters have to derive revenues from somewhere. Direct charges result in exclusion and significant welfare losses, yet they overcome the long-standing problem in broadcasting of the lack of signaling from consumers to suppliers. Pay television attracts more resources into the industry and, as the spread of digital technology and advances in the infrastructure for the Internet allow for an ever-widening number of channels, pay television will enable broadcasters to respond more closely to some patterns of viewer preference by supplying more varied output. However, if the costs and problems associated with exclusion are to be avoided, the two other main sources of funding – public support and advertising – will also have an important role to play in broadcasting in years ahead.

five

TELEVISION PRODUCTION

Building on the previous chapter, this one focuses on the economics of the upstream activity of content production and issues surrounding international trade in audiovisual content. The concept of 'windowing', and its importance as a business strategy for television programme-makers and other rights owners is examined. The significance of alternative financing models for rights creators is considered, drawing on the contrast between the 'deficit-financing' system favoured in the United States and the 'cost-plus' model which predominates in the UK television industry. The internationalization of the programme industry is considered and, drawing on relevant industrial arguments and international trade theory, the protectionist approach of the European Union is examined.

After studying this chapter, you should be able to:

- Understand the significance, for programme-makers, of strategies of deficit-financing and of windowing
- Explain the predominance of US suppliers in international trade of audiovisual product
- Analyse the response of European policy-makers
- Assess economic arguments for and against protectionism

ECONOMICS OF PROGRAMME SUPPLY

Decisions about which goods to produce and in what quantities are generally dictated by the interactions of producers and consumers. In the television industry, producers and consumers are connected via inter-mediary stages along a vertical supply chain. Typically, the programme 'packager' (often a broadcaster) plays a very important role in the supply chain, acting as an intermediary between programme-makers who have television content to sell and audiences who are interested in receiving television channels.

It is sometimes argued that, as patterns of television viewing become more personalized (thanks to the use of electronic programme guides, personal video recorders, etc.), self-scheduling may eventually displace the need for television channels (Brown, 1999: 17). As viewing patterns fragment, programmes rather than channels will become more important as brands and the modes of interaction between producers and consumers may be transformed. For now, however, it is generally not audiences *per se* but channel packagers and broadcasters who are the customers for television programming.

Production of media content is an expensive business. Each television programme, film, newspaper and magazine edition must offer messages, images or stories that are novel and unique. The persistent need for creative input – for novelty and innovation – makes content production a labour-intensive process. The production of commodities in the cultural industries as a whole (in arts as well as film, television, etc.) is said to suffer from 'Baumol's disease'[1] in that, because creativity is inherently labour-intensive and because labour costs tend to rise more quickly than others, costs in these sectors will tend to rise at a faster rate than inflation. Audiovisual content creation is particularly expensive because of the need for specialist capital (as well as human) resources such as cameras, studios, recording and editing equipment.

All in all, the expenses involved in generating the 'first copy' of any television programme tend to be considerable. But production costs vary widely between different categories or genres of programming and depending on quality. Table 5.1 provides a breakdown of average programming costs on the UK's most popular commercial television channel, ITV. This indicates the contrast between the costs of, for example, an hour of daytime programming (mainly studio-based discussion shows) and, at the far end of the scale, an hour of original television drama (which may involve large casts of actors, payments to script-writers, special sets and location shoots). Even within individual genres, production costs vary widely according to the quality and ambition of the programme. One hour of a costume drama, for example, may be considerably more expensive to make than an hour of a soap opera.

---

1. Named after US economist William J. Baumol.

TABLE 5.1 ITV network average cost per hour of original programming in 1999

Genre	Cost per hour (£000)
Drama	398
Entertainment	236
Documentaries	163
Arts & education	135
Children's	79
Late night	51
Religion	37
Daytime	18

Source: ITV Network Centre figures cited in Competition Commission, 2000: 106

Once the first copy of the programme has been created, it then costs little or nothing to reproduce and supply it to extra customers. As discussed earlier, the main value of television content is generally to do with attributes that are immaterial (i.e. its messages or meanings) and these do not get used up in the act of consumption. So, increasing marginal returns will be enjoyed as more and more customers for a television programme are added. The wider the audience for a programme, the more profitable it will become.

A key question for any media content production firm is who will reap the benefit (of reducing per-capita production costs) as consumption of its output expands? In the television industry, the powerful position occupied by dominant broadcasters may result in a situation where producers are unable to share in any of the benefits associated with the public-good attributes of their output. If, for example, broadcasters manage to purchase all the retransmission rights to the programmes they acquire from producers, then it is broadcasters and not producers who will benefit from all economies of scale that arise should that programming be sold to additional audiences.

The issue of rights ownership is crucial in the creative industries. The experience of many creators of intellectual property who have achieved financial success underlines the importance of retaining copyright and of exploiting rights as fully as possible. The ability of producers to exploit copyright effectively may depend on how market power is distributed along the vertical supply chain that stretches between the producer and the consumer. Theoretically, all of the different stages along the way are interdependent – e.g. distribution facilities are no good without supplies of content, and vice versa. But, in reality, strategic bottlenecks and concentrations of market power can develop. The problem both for producers and for distributors is that a monopolist or dominant player at any other stage along the supply chain may be able to appropriate some or all of their profits.

In the television production sector, a distinction can be drawn between two alternative models of financing which, in turn, have important implications for rights ownership. The term **deficit financing** describes a system, prevalent in the USA, where programme-makers share a portion of the financial risks involved in production in return for ownership of secondary and tertiary rights to their programmes (Litman, 1998: 140). Thus, producers (rather than broadcasters) can exploit their own hit programmes. By contrast, UK broadcasters tend to pay all production costs, so that producers are not exposed to any financial risk, but in return broadcasters retain the majority of secondary rights.

Deficit financing works in the following way. In return for the right to transmit a programme made by independent producers, the US networks systematically offer a fee which is less than the production budget for that programme, often by as much as one-third (Litman, 1998: 149). Programme-makers have to make up the difference or deficit. So programme producers are obliged to take a share in the financial risk associated with a new programme. If the programme flops then the producer loses out on the share of the production budget he or she has invested in it, because the programme has little or no residual value in secondary markets. On the other hand, if the programme is a hit, then the programme-maker stands to gain significantly from selling their programmes again either to other broadcasters in the US (a process known as secondary syndication), or to video distributors, or to overseas broadcasters. Secondary syndication to cable and satellite broadcasters, which is possible once a programme has had a successful first run on the main networks and once a sufficient number of episodes have been made, can provide substantial revenues for US programme-makers.

The deficit-financing model in the USA contrasts sharply with the **cost plus** system which prevails in the UK. Under the UK system, broadcasters who commission programmes from independent producers are prepared to cover the production budget in full and also to pay the programme-maker a small up-front production fee or profit, usually of around 10 per cent of the total production budget. However, in return, the broadcaster acquires not only the primary rights (or first right to transmit the programme) but also, generally, the majority of secondary rights (e.g. for additional transmissions on domestic television, video distribution and overseas sales).

The pattern of apportionment of risks and profits between broadcasters and programme-makers has important implications for the financial performance of both sectors. In the UK, independent producers have increasingly recognized that financial success requires participation in the risks and rewards of their output and have lobbied for change in the existing cost-plus arrangements (Woodward, 1998: 18). They complain that for years broadcasters have

> tried wherever possible to control all rights in a programme 'brand' (including copyright, distribution rights, trademarks, secondary rights and other rights not directly connected to broadcasting) when in fact all they have really needed is a right to broadcast. (Gutteridge et al., 2000: 3)

When content creators are left without any ownership of secondary rights, they have little or no economic incentive to build up and exploit their programme brands, for example by developing formats suitable for new media. Yet independent programme producers in the UK find that broadcasters rarely seem concerned with making the most of the secondary rights associated with the programmes they have acquired. If the system were changed so that content-creators were allowed to retain more of the secondary rights associated with their own programmes then, according to some producers, these rights would be exploited more efficiently and millions of pounds' worth of exports could be added every year.

Lack of participation in the rewards of success is undoubtedly a problem for independent producers in the UK. However, the cost-plus system shields producers from the financial risks associated with programmes that fail to cover their costs. In order to secure greater ownership of the secondary and tertiary rights to the programmes they create, such programme-makers would be required to share some portion of the financial risks involved, as do their counterparts in the USA. Since the majority of the thousand or so firms that currently comprise the television production sector in the UK are relatively small and under-capitalized, participation in a system of deficit financing would not necessarily prove that easy for most.

In fact, deficit financing in the USA tends to act as a barrier to market entry in the television production industry. The requirement to part-finance production expenses for programmes that may not recover their costs calls for substantial resources. Producers often lose money on series that are cancelled early by the major US networks, but 'such losses will be more than offset by huge profits on the occasionally highly successful show such as *M*A*S*H*, *Dallas*, *Seinfeld* or *ER*' (Hoskins et al., 1997: 76). To participate successfully in such strategies of cross-subsidization and risk-spreading, production companies need to be of a certain size and to have 'a portfolio of programs of different vintages in their inventory' (Litman, 1998: 135).

WINDOWING

The history and structure of the television production sector varies from one country to another and US producers enjoy a number of unique advantages over their rivals elsewhere. Consequently, the business of supplying programmes tends to be much more commercially advanced in the US than in other countries. The approach taken by US programme-makers to maximize the returns from ownership of programme rights is sometimes called windowing. Owen and Wildman (1992: 26) explain how programme suppliers try to maximize the exploitation of programme assets by regarding primary, secondary and tertiary television audiences as different 'windows'. The business of supplying programmes is about trying to maximize the value of your products by selling them not only through as many avenues or windows as possible but also in the pattern or order that yields the greatest return.

Content-suppliers set out to maximize the profits that can be earned from repeated showings of their output by carefully arranging the sequence and timing for releases of their work into the various distribution channels available. Figure 5.1. gives an example of the sorts of windows a television programme supplier will consider, although the exact order in which windows are ranked depends on the size of the audience that each makes available and the profit margin per viewer in each case. For UK producers, the most important domestic television windows are the free-to-air terrestrial channels, followed by cable or satellite distributed channels (which may be categorized as 'premium' or 'basic', depending on sub-scription charges). In the USA, the most important channels are the major terrestrial networks, the cable and satellite networks (pay, basic and pay-per-view) and independent stations.

Windowing is a form of price discrimination in that it involves the same product being sold at different prices to different groups of consumers for reasons not associated with differences in costs (Moschandreas, 1994:

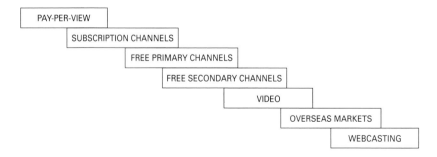

FIGURE 5.1   Possible distribution channels or windows for television programming

225). The total value that is placed on being able to watch a particular television programme will vary from individual to individual and it may also vary across time. Because the size of consumers' surplus for access to programmes varies among individual viewers and over time, a uniform viewing charge will not allow suppliers to maximize their income. A uniform charge that is too low would imply that only a small part of the audience's consumers' surplus is transferred to the supplier. But a uniform fee that is too high drives out of the market those viewers whose surplus is lower than the charge. Selling the programme at a different price to each viewer – a practice known as 'first degree price discrimination' – is clearly impractical. However, price discrimination between different groups of viewers or different distribution channels or windows – a form of 'third degree' price discrimination – is both practical and highly advantageous to the programme supplier.

Each showing of a television programme will reduce the earnings it can attract in subsequent releases in the same geographic market. As more viewers are exposed to a programme through one distribution channel they must simultaneously be eliminated from the potential audience that remains via other channels. In addition, the amount that purchasers will be prepared to pay for access to a particular programme tends to decline each time it gets an airing. So, generally speaking, channels with high per-viewer profit margins need to be scheduled early in the release sequence and ahead of releases to channels with lower per-viewer margins (Owen and Wildman, 1992: 33).

The size of the audience reached by a channel is another important factor that needs to be taken into account. If per-viewer profit margins are the same in all windows then the best strategy will be to schedule large audiences before small ones. This is because the 'real' value of money gradually diminishes over time. A payment of £100,000 which is due in 18 months' time is worth less than if it were received (and starting to accumulate bank interest) today. The aim for producers is to maximize the current day value of all potential revenue streams from showings of their output so the actual timing as well as the size of payments associated with each window will influence their place in the release sequence.

Third-degree price discrimination is feasible 'only if markets can be effectively segregated so that resale from the lower to the higher priced market is not possible' (Moschandreas, 1994: 227). It would be impossible to charge different prices to different audience segments for the same television show if those purchasing at the lower price could easily resell it to viewers at higher prices. Television markets are generally well segregated so that few circumstances exist where resale of transmission rights between purchasers is feasible. On the other hand, television broadcasts, video cassettes and digital video discs are vulnerable to illegal copying.

Piracy can result in the loss of significant potential revenues from secondary and tertiary markets so one of the issues a profit-maximizing content-producer must take into account in organizing its windowing strategy is how prone each distributive outlet or window is to illegal copying.

Windowing affects programme budgets, with extra potential cumulative revenue in a number of windows justifying a larger budget than would be feasible if a programme were released in just one distribution channel. A television series can be highly profitable even though none of the individual windows it sells through would, on its own, provide sufficient revenues to cover the costs of production. Production decisions often reflect the various distributive outlets a production firm is targeting. Sometimes a particular actor or story-line is fed into a television production precisely because that element is expected to increase the attractiveness of the programme for audiences in a specific window. For example, the inclusion of a popular actor from the USA in a European television production might be designed to ensure that the programme will be purchased by US television channels.

So, windowing involves not only domestic outlets but also overseas ones. To maximize the value of their assets, programme suppliers need to devise a strategy for exploiting all available transmission and other rights in as many territories as possible across the globe. Overseas markets represent increasingly important windows for television content, as is evidenced by the popularity in the UK and elsewhere of imported television programmes such as *Friends* and *Frasier*. The prices that broadcasters are willing (and able to afford) to pay in different geographic markets for, say, the same half-hour comedy show vary widely. A wide discrepancy exists between, for example, what European broadcasters and African broadcasters are willing to pay for an hour of US programming (Hoskins et al., 1997: 69). Consequently, in order to maximize international revenues, programme suppliers need to discriminate on price between different overseas territories as well as between primary and secondary markets.

As well as gaining income through the sale of television transmission rights in various release windows, creators of successful programme brands may also be able to derive revenues from ancillary markets by the exploitation of copyright in related and complementary goods. This is especially true for children's television programming, where many internationally renowned character brands have been created, such as *Scooby Doo* and *The Simpsons*. The BBC's *Teletubbies* series has given rise to vast revenues for the BBC from licensing the sale of a wide array of videos, books, magazines, toys and other merchandise bearing the Teletubbies brand. Another high-profile success for UK television content-makers is the *Bob the Builder* children's programme which was developed by the BBC and HIT Entertainment in the late 1990s. The broadcasting rights to *Bob the Builder* have now been sold in 108 countries and the strength of the brand created by the television programme has resulted in a variety of lucrative spin-off products, including books, toys, clothing and a CD-Rom (White, 2000: 21).

INTERNATIONAL TRADE IN AUDIOVISUAL CONTENT

The spread of cable, satellite and, more recently, digital compression techniques has facilitated a continuous expansion in the way in which television can be distributed to viewers. The proliferation of new television channels has had a major impact on the broadcasting system. Greater distribution capacity and lower distribution costs have reduced entry barriers in broadcasting and led to greater competition. As far as television producers are concerned, one of the most significant implications is that the need for television content has increased dramatically.

In the UK, the four analogue terrestrial television channels which existed in 1988 then transmitted a total of around 70 hours of television per day between them. A decade later, the average number of terrestrial television hours had increased to over 100 per day because of additional daytime and late-night transmissions and the arrival of one extra player, Channel 5. More significantly, growth in the number of cable and satellite channels broadcasting in the UK was exponential in the 1990s. Cable, satellite and digital terrestrial broadcasting have swelled the total number of hours of television transmitted every day in the UK in 2001 to well over a thousand.

Channel proliferation is an international phenomenon. The number of cable and satellite channels operating in Europe grew from fewer than 100 in 1990 to in excess of 600 in 1998 and the pace of expansion is on the increase (see Figure 5.2). The use of digital broadcasting technology has begun to spread throughout Europe since the late 1990s and digital compression techniques mean that as many as ten channels may now be transmitted within the same bandwidth as was previously required for just one analogue channel. So the number of television services continues to expand rapidly and this has brought about an explosive growth in the number of television hours transmitted daily. The worldwide need for attractive television content is growing quickly.

Suppliers of television content have gained considerably from this trend. According to data collected by *Screen Digest*, the total value of television programme sales to both free and pay-television channels across Europe grew from just under $2 billion in 1995 to around $3.5 billion in 1999

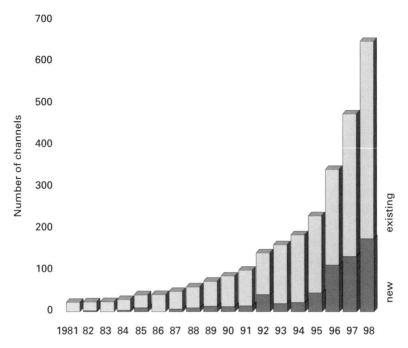

FIGURE 5.2   Growth of European cable and satellite channels, 1981–98 (Screen Digest, in Brown, 1999: 12)

– an increase of more than 75 per cent in just four years (2000a: 117). Analysis of trends in international trade in audiovisual products confirms that many of the additional hours on new television channels are filled with imported programming, much of it from the USA.

Many successful cable and satellite channels start out by relying quite heavily on relatively inexpensive acquired and imported programming. Second-hand programmes with 'a record of beating competition, a history of drawing large and broad audiences, and a sufficient inventory of episodes' are particularly attractive (Carveth et al., 1998: 226). However, as commercial television channels mature, they tend to transmit fewer hours of imported programming, especially during peak time. As new channels gain more income, they may switch from imports to domestic acquisitions or even to making original programming (Brown, 1999: 40).

Foreign programmes are generally subject to a 'cultural discount' – i.e. they sell for less than domestically made programmes of the same type – which reflects the natural preference of viewers for content made in their own home markets and in their languages and accents (Hoskins et al., 1997: 32–3). Even so, many imported programmes offer excellent value for money to broadcasters, so imports remain central to the overall schedules of most cable and satellite channels in Europe. Germany, which has a rapidly growing and highly competitive pay-television sector, is currently the largest market in Europe for imported programming in terms of total annual expenditure (Screen Digest, 2000a: 119). Broadcasters in the UK, France and Italy are also major purchasers of acquired and imported programming.

The fact that there is such a large volume of international trade in audiovisual products can be accounted for by the public-good characteristics of the commodity. The low to zero marginal cost of supplying television content to additional viewers in another market means that second-hand programming tends to be available in plentiful supplies and traded at prices which are attractive to an importing broadcaster. As far as the importer is concerned, acquiring single transmission rights for overseas television programmes is usually a very much cheaper option than commissioning the production of original material. Hoskins et al. (1997: 80) suggest that a Canadian broadcaster can acquire an imported drama series (from the US) for around one-tenth of the cost of producing it itself in-house. Likewise, the cost for a UK broadcaster of acquiring an imported drama (which, in 1999, cost as little as $40,000 per hour) is a fraction of the average cost per hour of making original drama.

The buoyancy of international markets for television content reflects how cost-effective second-hand programming can be in a broadcaster's schedule. Channel 5 in the UK, for example, spends around 10 per cent of its annual programme budget (of £120 million) on acquired programmes, but these programmes account for around 30–40 per cent of its revenues.[2] Many UK cable and satellite channels rely heavily on acquired and imported programmes, partly because second-hand programmes are all they can afford but also because second-hand programmes provide a higher rate of return than original productions, in terms of audiences generated for each pound spent.

As far as the cost differential between acquired content and original television productions is concerned, it is essential to distinguish between what exactly is being paid for in each case. A broadcaster that imports a programme will usually pay a fee in return for single transmission rights in its own territory. On the other hand, a broadcaster that pays for an original programme to be produced (either in-house or by an independent programme-maker) will usually acquire a stake in all the transmission and reproduction rights associated with that programme brand in all territories across the globe. So, as Noam puts it (1993: 41), to compare the price of imported programmes and domestic productions is like comparing a

---

2. Figures cited by David Elstein, then Chief Executive of Channel 5, during a guest lecture to the MSc in Media Management class at the University of Stirling on 8 October 1999.

taxi fare with the cost of a new car. An importing broadcaster acquires transmission rights in one window only whereas the producer of a new programme acquires a commodity that has residual value in several alternative windows.

THE DOMINANCE OF US TELEVISION SUPPLIERS

The strength of US producers in international audiovisual trade (i.e. films and television programmes) is well documented. The factors that give the US 'majors' such a predominant position in global markets for feature films are examined in the following chapter. Markets for television programmes, as distinct from movies, tend to be much more pluralistic and reliant on domestic producers. Nonetheless, US suppliers also occupy a leading position as exporters of regular television content. According to data compiled by *Screen Digest*, US suppliers accounted for 'the lion's share' of all expenditure on 'acquired' programmes by European television broadcasters throughout the late 1990s (Screen Digest, 2000a: 118).

There are several reasons for this. The historical development of the Hollywood-based production industry in the US is unique and television programme-makers have clearly benefited from regulatory interventions aimed at curbing the power of dominant broadcasters. The Financial Interest and Syndication rules, which were in place from 1970 until 1995, forced the three major television networks (ABC, CBS and NBC) to source a high proportion of their output from independent television content-makers. This has facilitated the development of an exceptionally mature and well-funded production sector in the US.

In addition, the size of the domestic market provides a major competitive advantage for US programme suppliers. In 2000 there were some 99 million television households in the USA as compared with, say, 24 million in the UK. 'The US enjoys the unique combination of a large population with a common language and high per capita income, which makes it the biggest of the world's markets for television programmes, feature films and videos' (Hoskins et al., 1997: 38). Smaller markets cannot benefit from the economies of scale that can be achieved in the US television market.

A key advantage of the large and relatively affluent domestic US television audience is that it makes available more resources for the production of television programming. Levels of GDP per capita in the US, at $30,000 in 1996–97, are marginally ahead of both Germany and France and some 33 per cent ahead of the UK (Oliver, 2000: 61). Domestic expenditure on newly originated television programming in the US, at $63 per capita in 1996–97, is also much higher than in other countries (ibid.). So not only is the US audience large and wealthy, but US viewers are prepared to spend more per head on consuming domestically made programmes than are viewers elsewhere.

A considerable pool of revenue is available to support commercial television production in the USA. Secondary and tertiary broadcasting markets are well developed and US programme suppliers are generally adept in pursuing strategies that exploit all available windows effectively. The greater resources available to television producers in the USA has facilitated the development of large enterprises capable of part-financing production expenses on shows commissioned by networks. Large scale producers are able to engage in strategies of cross-subsidization and can spread their risks more effectively across a range of total output. Greater resources also mean larger production budgets and this allows US programme-makers to include more costly elements (such as high-profile actors, special effects, etc.) that, in turn, lead to strong programme brands and a wide audience appeal.

US television producers benefit from the fact that English is an international language. Norwegian and Greek television producers cannot hope to compete in international markets with the predominance of US suppliers because few television audiences will put up with programming in foreign languages, especially minority languages. The advantage of making products in the English language is shared by producers in the UK, Australia, Canada and Ireland but, except for the UK, these countries have achieved relatively little success as exporters of programming. According to industry estimates, the UK is the only country in the world, apart from the USA, that has a net trade surplus in television programme rights (Oliver, 2000: 60–1). The BBC is, in fact, by far the largest exporter of programmes in Europe (Hydra Associates, 1996: 60). But the estimated UK surplus of some £16 million in 1997 is dwarfed by the US trade surplus in television programming of well in excess of $2 billion in 1994 (Carveth et al., 1998: 230). So language alone is by no means a sufficient factor to explain the dominance of US programme suppliers.

Advantages of audience size, audience wealth and language are reinforced by the high concentration of television production resources, personnel and specialist support services in the US home market. Programme-makers can take advantage of an extensive local talent pool and production centres that are highly resourced, especially in Los Angeles. Local conditions in the USA are clearly conducive to successful television programme-making whereas many other markets lack a comparable infrastructure and comparable levels of locally based talent and expertise.

Moreover, since production costs will usually be recouped in the home market, US television programmes are available to the export market at low cost. It makes sense for broadcasters to pay a low cost for imported US programmes that are likely to prove acceptable or even highly appealing (e.g. *Friends*, *Frasier* or *ER*) to domestic audiences rather than to produce original programming themselves. The large supply of relatively inexpensive second-hand programming churned out by the US television industry each year means that broadcasters and audiences around the globe can share in some of the benefits of low marginal supply costs for television content.

It is sometimes argued that this amounts to 'dumping' by US programme suppliers. Dumping occurs where a good is sold in an overseas market at a price below the real cost of production. It is generally frowned upon as a practice because of its damaging effects on local producers. In the case of television exports, the good is almost certainly sold into foreign markets at a price well below initial production costs. But the price at which the programme is sold is bound to be well above the marginal cost of supplying it (i.e. the cost of making and supplying one extra copy of the original to the importing broadcaster). So, whether or not programme exports correspond with the technical description of dumping depends on which definition of 'cost' is used. Since what is being sold is not the programme *per se* but merely the right to transmit it in one territory, marginal costs seem in some ways to provide the more relevant benchmark.

The perception of US producers dumping product onto foreign markets also overlooks the fact that programme-makers often set out with the intention of recouping their costs not just through domestic primary and secondary sales but also through a series of releases into additional geographic markets. The US domestic market is large but it may not necessarily provide all the revenue needed to ensure that a television programme will be produced. The targeting of international markets may sometimes play an important part in a producer's windowing strategy, to the extent that international preferences exert some influence over production decisions (Noam, 1993: 47). Spreading production costs across as many different release windows and territories as possible is, after all, the fundamental recipe for success for any media content-producer.

One of the questions that has exercised the minds of Europe's audio-visual policy-makers is why can't European programme-makers take advantage of the large and affluent domestic European television audience in the same way as US suppliers exploit their own home market? Why is it that European programme suppliers seem unable to employ windowing strategies with the same success as their US counterparts? There are some 130 million television households in Western Europe as compared with 99 million in the USA, and national broadcasters across Europe generate a great deal of second-hand programming every year. The problem, however, is that very little of it seems to be of any interest to broadcasters in other countries.

One obvious barrier to cross-border trade in television programmes in Europe is language. Audiences in each of Europe's main television markets – Germany, France, Spain, Italy and the UK – have a preference for product made in their own language. It can also be argued that cultural variations are much more pronounced throughout Europe than in the USA and so there is really no such thing as a pan-European audience. Europe may call itself a 'single market' but, when it comes to the exchange of media and other cultural goods, it still tends to behave like a collection of many distinctive markets.

Another factor militating against exports of European programming is that most important television players in Europe, unlike their US rivals, have grown out of a tradition of public service rather than commercial broadcasting. Hoskins et al. suggest that 'much of the competition [for US television suppliers] in international markets has been from in-house production by public broadcast monopolies not well versed in producing programmes people want to watch' (1997: 44). Europe's public broadcasters have, naturally enough, tended to concentrate their efforts on the needs and interests of domestic audiences rather than on potential for exporting programmes to international markets. Since the early 1990s, increased competition within broadcasting has encouraged European broadcasters and programme-makers to become more outward-looking and competitive. Even so, US content-suppliers continue to predominate; as a consequence, the European Union (EU) was running an annual trade deficit in audiovisual products (i.e. television programmes plus feature films) with the USA of some $5 billion in 2000.

'FORTRESS EUROPE': THE QUOTAS

While the UK has just about managed to maintain a positive trade balance in television rights, a one-way traffic flow coming from the US is much more typical of the pattern of trade in audiovisual content across Europe. This has raised concerns on both economic and cultural grounds. In economic terms, the most obvious problems for Europe are a negative trade balance and lack of employment and wealth creation in its own indigenous production sectors. As far as culture is concerned, the 'invasion' of foreign television content is perceived by some as posing a threat to indigenous languages and values.

Europe has responded by putting into place a number of collective policy initiatives and funding schemes intended to support the position of indigenous European television producers *vis-à-vis* their US rivals. For example, the European Commission has operated several public funding schemes since the 1980s that have subsidized or supported production, co-production and, particularly, distribution of European-made television programmes across different member states of the EU. The MEDIA Plus initiative which came into operation in 2001 involves direct subsidies targeted at three 'priority' areas identified by the Commission. These are training for audiovisual professionals, development of European productions with cross-border appeal and distribution of new audiovisual works by European producers.[3] The main rationale for these support measures is that European societies will collectively benefit from positive externalities if European viewers are exposed to more indigenous programming.

But the main policy measure used to protect the European television production industry from US imports is the compulsory European programming quota contained in a Directive entitled *Television without Frontiers*. *Television without Frontiers* (TWF) or 'The Broadcasting Directive' of 1997 (97/36/EC) was originally agreed by member states in 1989 and its basic aim was to ensure that broadcast service providers can take advantage of the European single market by being legally able to operate across frontiers in much the same way as service providers in any other industry. One of the fundamental principles of TWF is that broadcast services should comply with one and only one national law, i.e. the law of the national state from which they 'originate'. They are then free to circulate in all the member states of the EU in much the same way as, say, a car driver can use his or her licence to drive around Europe without having to pass a driving test in each country. But compliance with a minimum set of common rules and standards is required and TWF sets out common rules in four main areas: the protection of minors, viewers' right of reply, advertising and the so-called 'quotas'.

Designed to protect the indigenous programme-making industry, the compulsory quota for European-made content obliges all EU broadcasters to ensure that at least 50 per cent of their transmitted output is of European origin. Article 4 of TWF says:

> Member States shall ensure where practicable and by appropriate means, that broadcasters reserve for European works . . . a majority proportion of their transmission time, excluding the time appointed to news, sports events, games, advertising and teletext services. This proportion . . . should be achieved progressively, on the basis of suitable criteria. (CEC, 1997)

---

3. Details of European support schemes can be found on the European Commission's Audiovisual Policy homepage at http://europa.eu.int/comm/avpolicy/avpolicy.index_en.htm

The European quota is criticized as being 'protectionist' by US television exporters. It is also unpopular with many European broadcasters and, generally, is not properly enforced by member state authorities. Quotas have been criticized as being too arbitrary and an ineffective way of supporting the sort of indigenous content which creates external benefits (Hoskins et al., 1997: 97). A more general criticism of import controls and quotas is that they 'deny consumers foreign products that they would otherwise have consumed because of their superior price or performance characteristics relative to domestically produced products' (Collins et al., 1988: 52).

The most widely heard objection to the European content quotas concerns their effect on broadcasters' operating costs. If European broadcasters are forced to buy 50 per cent of their programmes from domestic suppliers then, because domestic prices are typically higher than import prices (for the same performance characteristics), this will have a depressing effect on the total number of hours which broadcasters can afford to buy. Because of higher domestic programme prices, quotas increase the cost for broadcasters of acquiring programme material to fill up their schedules. Assuming that broadcasters within Europe are subject to budgetary constraints, then the effect of the quota is twofold. First, it reduces the overall level of demand for programmes . Second, it redistributes demand in favour of domestic producers.

Any positive redistribution of demand in favour of European programme-makers clearly represents a benefit for the European production industry, at least in the short term. On the other hand, quotas (if they were properly enforced) would increase broadcasters' costs and depress the overall level of demand for programming. In other words, with properly enforced quotas, fewer hours of programming could be paid for and so a smaller number of television services are feasible than under 'free market' conditions.

In the absence of quotas, new channels will undoubtedly tend to rely on inexpensive US imports, at least initially. But as commercial television channels mature and gain increased audiences and revenues, there is a natural tendency to substitute domestic acquisitions for imports because most audiences exhibit a preference for domestic programmes. Consequently, it may be argued, the long-term interests of domestic programme producers will be better served if broadcasting markets are allowed to flourish without quotas. Extra growth in the market will bring more not less demand for domestic programming.

So, opposition to the European quota in *TWF* has been based on concerns that strict enforcement would slow down expansion in the number of new channels operating across Europe, thus narrowing consumer choice and reducing demand for European programmes in the long term. It is argued that the additional expense involved in acquiring attractive European-made as opposed to US programmes would force new broadcast channels out of the market and deter others from entering. Quotas would give domestic programme-makers a higher market share, but their gains would be offset by the fact that domestic broadcasting markets would be growing much more slowly. European producers suffer from the lack of healthy and mature secondary and tertiary domestic markets or windows to sell their programmes into. Thus, to impose strict quotas and choke off the growth of new channels might actually be counter-productive, as far as domestic producers are concerned.

Proponents of the compulsory European quota argue that the best way to strengthen our indigenous production sector is to ensure that all broadcasters in Europe acquire a reasonable proportion of their output from European producers. This would raise broadcasters' costs and might well force new entrants out of the market or deter others from entering but it would also ensure that European producers get some share of the benefits of an expanding market, rather than allowing the US production industry to consolidate its dominant worldwide position. In addition, the compulsory European quota helps Europe's balance of trade in audiovisual products and services.

So, quota policies are seen by some as a pro- rather than an anti-competitive force. The television industry is prone to oligopoly and so interventions that improve the position of smaller players in countries other than the USA will serve to 'restore' rather than distort competition in European markets (Renaud, 1993: 154). In any event, it may be argued that 'market forces are not necessarily synonymous with the consumer interest' (ibid.), especially when it comes to cultural industries. In addition to such economic arguments that exist in favour of protecting domestic production industries, many proponents of the compulsory European quota point to the cultural implications of allowing domestic television production to become marginalized.

PROTECTIONISM VERSUS FREE INTERNATIONAL TRADE

International trade in cultural output gets caught at the crossroads between conflicting socio-political, cultural and economic interests. The public-good characteristics of media content – the fact that however many times it is consumed it does not get used up – means that, unlike most products, it can be sold over and over and over again to new audiences. Reproduction costs are negligible and scarcity is not a problem. So media content seems well suited to wide international distribution. From a producer's point of view, spreading production costs across as many additional geographic markets as possible is the ideal strategy.

At the same time, however, any threat to indigenous producers of cultural output tends to bring out 'protective' impulses. Notwithstanding language barriers, domestic European television producers often find it difficult to compete in their own home markets with attractive, high-budget second-hand programme exports from the USA which are readily available at a low cost. Profit-seeking broadcasters will naturally want to use this supply of inexpensive programming. This places domestic producers at a perceived disadvantage. Concerns about the need for indigenous programming and the potential harm to indigenous cultures, languages and values that may be caused by high levels of import penetration television have been central to European debates about audiovisual policy.

But the invocation of cultural concerns is sometimes regarded as a disguise for straightforward, old-fashioned protectionism. Television production is a major international business, employing tens of thousands of individuals across the globe and generating billions of pounds in commercial revenue every year not only for US suppliers but for producers in many other countries too. Some would argue that television is not really that different from any other business sector so the use of subsidies, quotas or other special measures to prop up local producers is not only unnecessary but is also wasteful.

To analyse the arguments for and against protection of indigenous producers, it is worth understanding some of the fundamentals of international trade theory. The basic theory of 'gains from trade' was developed by David Ricardo in 1817. Ricardo was extending Adam Smith's earlier notion about the benefits of division of labour to a global level. Smith observed that specialization of labour – the allocation of different jobs to different people on the basis of what each person does best – and voluntary exchange of goods and services is a much more efficient way of organizing things than expecting everyone to be self-sufficient. Modern economies are based on this notion of specialization and division of labour. Ricardo took the idea further by suggesting that each country should specialize in those goods which it can produce most efficiently, e.g. Brazil should produce coffee, Scotland should produce sheep, etc.

With free international trade, each country or region can concentrate on producing whatever it happens to be good at making or whatever it produces most cost-efficiently. If each area specializes in producing commodities for which it has some natural or acquired advantage and buys in whatever it does not produce efficiently from other countries, then the world's limited resources will be used as efficiently as possible and, in theory, everyone can enjoy a higher standard of living. But what happens if one country is more efficient than another in the production of all goods? Ricardo pointed out that there are still gains to be made (i.e. world output will be maximized) so long as each country specializes in whatever it is relatively good at producing or whatever it happens to have a 'comparative advantage' in and then we trade with each other freely.

Does the USA have a comparative advantage in television production? The traditional notion of comparative advantage relies on the assumption that certain countries or regions are inherently better suited to producing some commodities rather than others, probably because of endowments of natural resources or local climatic conditions. A competing view is that comparative advantages are not necessarily nature-given and fixed but are, in fact, acquired and may change over time. The USA is clearly the world's most successful exporter of audiovisual goods and services. Yet most of the major factors involved in production of television programming (particularly the human capital) seem to be internationally mobile rather than fixed. So its comparative advantage may, to a large extent, be acquired rather than naturally occurring.

The fact that television production in the USA results in English language product is certainly one major factor which inherently favours US suppliers, as it does producers in other English-speaking countries including the UK, Canada and Ireland. The size and wealth of the domestic market is also a major advantage for US television producers: the ability to spread production costs over such an enormous home market means that US producers are able to offer television programmes to overseas audiences at extremely competitive prices.

But if the economies of scale available in the US market were enough to guarantee international success for its television producers, then why don't US producers predominate in all areas of cultural production? Why is it that in pop music, for example, UK producers have managed to become a more important international force? Evidently, US audiovisual producers have some special flair for creating output with a wide appeal that is not fully shared by US producers of other forms of cultural output.

Television producers in the USA also benefit from a concentration of talent, technical equipment and specialist support services related to audiovisual production. However, these are acquired rather than natural resources. Judging by its current trade surplus, it appears that the USA does indeed enjoy a comparative advantage in production of television content. But natural endowments of raw materials or climate cannot adequately account for this.

If relatively few of the factors which contribute to the USA's comparative advantage in television production are innate and immutable, this implies that other countries could similarly acquire a comparative advantage over time. Theoretically, many of the USA's advantages in television production are contestable. But in reality it would be foolish to assume that the conditions which currently favour US television suppliers in international markets could easily be replicated elsewhere.

The desire to build indigenous audiovisual production players that are competitive in home and in world markets has resulted in the use of a variety of methods of protection in different countries over the years. One commonly used method is to offer subsidies of various kinds to domestic producers so as to improve their competitiveness in both the home and world markets. Tariffs provide another example. These are taxes levied on imported television programmes or films. Tariffs protect indigenous producers by increasing the costs of imports and they provide a source of revenue for the Government. Quotas – such as the one set out in Article 4 of *TWF* – are another means of limiting imports and boosting demand for the output of local producers.

According to international trade theory, the introduction of any artificial support measures to encourage local production of a commodity – cultural or otherwise – which can be created more cheaply or cost-efficiently elsewhere will lead to a sub-optimal use of resources. The use of special policies to develop indigenous industries that do not have, and will never achieve, comparative advantages is generally a waste of time. Protectionism may serve the interests of domestic producers but encouraging high-cost local production inevitably results in a misallocation of resources, with concomitant welfare losses. Another major drawback of such measures is that they invite the prospect of retaliation.

There may, however, be some situations when a degree of selective protectionism is justified. For example, when dumping occurs then a typical response is to impose a tariff. But the practice of selling programmes in overseas markets at below their initial production costs cannot accurately be described as dumping. Another situation where protectionism is considered justifiable is in order to nurture an 'infant industry'. The use of protective measures to help establish new industries is widely accepted and, indeed, is explicitly provided for under Article 18 of the General Agreement on Tariffs and Trade or GATT – an international institution created specifically to foster trade (Griffiths and Wall, 1999: 642). If there is a belief that a period of time is required for the local industry to 'move along a learning curve' until it becomes fully competitive then there would be a valid argument for protecting the industry for a limited period until it matures and becomes competitive in the international market and no longer needs protection.

Whether or not this sort of argument is applicable to European television production industries is debatable. The most obvious disadvantage for European programme-makers is that they operate in much smaller domestic markets than US programme-makers, which makes it difficult for them to build up the same critical mass. Some scholars dismiss the use of infant industry arguments to support European quotas as illegitimate (Hoskins et al., 1997: 85–6). Production of television programmes is by no means a 'new' activity in most developed countries so the retention of subsidies and other protective intervention for extended periods cannot really be justified on the grounds of temporarily supporting an infant industry.

Other arguments in favour of protection of domestic television producers focus on the fact that patterns of trade in media products have important cultural implications. The availability of domestically made audiovisual content creates positive externalities (beneficial side-effects for society, including a strengthened sense of community, etc.). So, for example, even if Hollywood has a comparative advantage in making English-language programmes because of economies of scale in a market as large as the USA, this does not necessarily imply that the UK should just give up domestic television production and import all its programmes. Protective measures for television producers can undoubtedly be justified on non-economic or cultural grounds.

During the Uruguay round of GATT negotiations, European negotiators argued that audiovisual goods and services require special protection from free international trade. The trade talks almost came unstuck in December 1993 because of a deadlock between the Motion Picture Exporters Association of America (MPEAA) and European trade negotiators who insisted that audiovisual services should be excluded from the negotiations on 'cultural' grounds (Jeancolas, 1998: 59). Not surprisingly, most US programme exporters tend to regard cultural arguments as a convenient smoke-screen for protectionism (Hoskins et al., 1997: 87). But, in the final GATT agreement, European trade negotiators succeeded in securing a 'cultural exclusion' for audiovisual goods and services. Nonetheless, Europe's protectionist stance on film and television continues to provoke attacks from US exporters' trade associations and is certain to remain a contentious issue during future rounds of trade talks.

six

THE INTERNATIONAL FILM INDUSTRY

This chapter analyses the determinants of economic success in the film industry. The risk-reduction strategies of the major Hollywood studios are examined and explained. Concepts of industrial structure, vertical integration and market power are revisited, drawing on the distinction between 'majors' and 'independents' and on the contrasting examples provided by the European and United States film production and distribution sectors.

After studying this chapter, you should be able to:

- Understand the main sources of earnings available for feature films
- Explain the economic success of the major Hollywood studios
- Assess the importance of the distribution phase in the vertical supply chain for films
- Analyse the main obstacles to private sector investment in 'independent' film production

FILM REVENUES

To understand how the international film industry works, a good starting point is to consider the different sources of revenue for films. Cinema advertising in the UK and across Europe represents less than 1 per cent of total advertising expenditure so it is generally not a significant source of income for the film industry (Advertising Association, 2000: 6). Feature films earn the vast majority of their revenue from direct or indirect charges to consumers for access to the product. A handful of successful feature films also manage to generate some income in royalties from associated merchandising.

Films tend to earn most of their income in three categories of release window – cinema box-office (or 'theatrical'), video and television. The cinema box-office has traditionally been the main source of income but revenues from video (rentals and retail or 'sell-through') grew very strongly throughout the 1980s. Since the mid-1990s the proportion of film revenue accounted for by the television window has increased rapidly alongside growth in the number of movie-based subscription channels.

In most developed economies, consumer expenditure on watching feature films has been growing in all of these three main categories. In the UK, for example, expenditures at the box-office have been steadily increasing since the mid-1980s thanks to improving trends in cinema-going (Figure 6.1). UK cinema admissions in 1997 – at 139 million – were higher than in any other year since 1974. This upturn reverses an earlier pattern of long-term decline in cinema attendances starting in the 1950s when television first began to establish itself as the most popular form of mass entertainment. But going out to the cinema as a leisure activity has been increasing in popularity since the 1980s, not only in the UK but also in most other European countries and beyond.

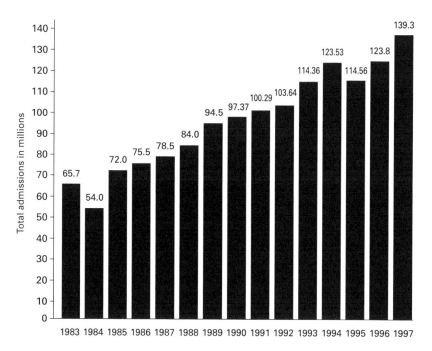

FIGURE 6.1   UK cinema admissions, 1983–97 (Entertainment Data Inc./Screen Digest/
Screen Finance cited in BFI, 1999: 29)

In the UK, the recovery in admissions is at least partly accounted for by heavy investment in increasing the total number of cinema screens. The number of multiplex cinema sites operating in the UK rose rapidly throughout the 1990s and the total amount of screens doubled from 1,271 to 2,564 between 1984 and 1998 (BFI, 1999: 31). The arrival of multi-screen, family-friendly cinema sites has naturally encouraged more expenditure at the UK box-office. Even so, average cinema attendances in the UK, at 2.1 per head of population in 1996, are still only half the level of the USA, where the frequency of cinema-going is 4.25 visits per annum (Clarke and Till, 1998: 36).

The performance of a film at the cinema or 'exhibition' phase has traditionally been very important in terms of earning revenue but, in fact, secondary and tertiary windows – video and subscription television – have emerged as even more lucrative sources of income for the film industry over the last decade or so. Nonetheless, the box-office performance of a film is still very significant because, even though films tend to earn more money at the video and television stages, it is in the cinema release window that a film tends to establish its popularity. The film's appeal or lack of appeal to audiences is discovered in the exhibition window. A film that fails to produce the desired results when first released theatrically is highly unlikely to achieve a wide release overseas and may, instead, go directly to a video release or straight to television. So a film's box-office performance has important knock-on effects in later distribution phases.

But, as a source of consumer expenditure on film, the cinema box-office has been well and truly overtaken by moneys spent on renting and buying videos. Video expenditure grew very strongly alongside the penetration of video cassette recorder (VCR) ownership in the 1980s. Rental started out as the main source of income from video and it remains so in many European countries, but in the UK direct retailing to the consumer of videos (not only of feature films but also of other special-interest television programming) has grown into a more important revenue earner.

Video accounted for the majority of UK film expenditure in the early 1990s but has now been overtaken by a relatively new source of income for films: subscriptions to television movie channels (see Table 6.1). Over the last decade, movie channels have come to represent an increasingly important form of consumer expenditure on films throughout Europe. The main distribution channels through which films are sold to consumers have changed considerably since the 1980s and they continue to evolve today with, for example, the emergence of video-on-demand (VOD) and digital video discs (DVDs) occupying a more central role in the distribution chain.

Per-viewer profit margins differ from one film to the next, depending on how successful the theatrical run has been and what price can be

TABLE 6.1   UK consumer expenditure on feature films, 1987-97 (£m)

	UK box-office	Video rental	Video retail*	Movie channel subscriptions	Total
1987	169	410	100	–	679
1988	193	470	175	–	838
1989	227	555	320	–	1,102
1990	273	550	365	47	1,235
1991	295	540	444	121	1,400
1992	291	511	400	283	1,485
1993	319	528	643	350	1,840
1994	364	438	698	540	2,040
1995	385	789	457	721	2,352
1996	426	491	803	1,003	2,723
1997	506	369	858	1,290	3,023

* Movies account for only a portion of the UK video retail market.

Source: BVA/EDI/BSkyB cited in BFI, 1999: 25

negotiated for rights in subsequent release windows. Profit margins also differ from one window to another and this affects the release sequence for a film. Using the same approach as suppliers of television content, distributors of a film will try to order the timing of successive releases into different windows in such a way as to maximize the total profits that can be earned from repeated showings of the film. A typical release sequence (see Figure 6.2) reflects the gradual and ongoing diminution in margins as the film moves from cinema through video to repeats on free-to-air television.

The US box-office tends to provide large revenues and high margins so theatrical release in the US is generally the first window (Gasson, 1996: 189). This is followed, typically some 2–3 months later, by theatrical release in other countries, including the UK. The overseas theatrical release window may stretch over a period of many months. Meanwhile, a short television pay-per-view (ppv) window may open up some 4–6 months after the film gets its first theatrical release and, immediately afterwards (perhaps some 6–9 months after first release), the film enters the worldwide home video window. Only after the film has had a chance to exhaust relatively

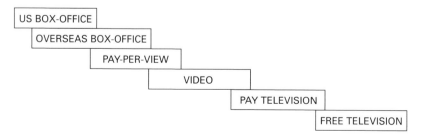

FIGURE 6.2   Typical sequence of windows for distribution of feature films

high-margin theatrical, ppv and video windows will it make its first appearance on television. The window for pay television channels starts to open up 12 months after the film's first release, and after a further 12 months or so it will appear on major free-to-air channels followed, some time later, by secondary free-to-air channels.

Merchandising provides another possible source of income, from the *Toy Story* mouse mat to *Jurassic Park* games and toys. Filmmakers that focus on children's entertainment are generally the main earners of income in ancillary markets. Disney has been particularly successful in exploiting opportunities to extend its character brands. Its theme parks generate significant revenues and Disney also profits from licensing the production of clothing, toys and a myriad of other products that derive value from an association with Disney film brands. Global retail sales of licensed merchandise are estimated to have reached some $112 billion in 1998 and, of this, around $29 billion represented sales of 'entertainment/ character' property types, which include film and television brand-licensing (Sanghera, 2000: 12).

Total spending on filmed entertainment in the UK, across European markets and in the USA has increased steadily throughout the 1980s and 1990s. However, a problem for the UK, as well as for other countries worldwide, is that the bulk of domestic consumer expenditure on films is generated by and ploughed back into the dominant Hollywood-based US film production industry. In the UK, some 84 per cent of box-office receipts in 1998 were accounted for by US films (BFI, 2000: 35). The imbalance in the video market is equally bad with some 80–90 per cent of video rentals in the UK each year accounted for by US film products. So, of the £3 billion or so spent by UK consumers on films every year (see Table 6.1) only a tiny proportion goes back into UK film production. Wholly British films accounted for just 4 per cent of the total UK box-office in 1998 (ibid.).

The film industry is very much an international business but, as far as Europe is concerned, it is a sector that is comprehensively dominated by the product of just one country – the USA. India is one of the few countries in the world with a strong enough indigenous commercial film industry to resist the domination of Hollywood. The number of films produced in India in 1999 was 764 as compared with 628 films made in the US and 92 films made in the UK in the same year, making India 'the world's most prolific film-producing nation'(Screen Digest, 2000b: 181). But in the UK and the rest of Europe, US films rule. Across Europe, US-made films account for an average of no less than 70 per cent of total cinema admissions (2000a: 189)

THE US MODEL

A small handful of multinational companies account for the overwhelming success of US films in world markets. The US industry is made up of two branches: the 'major' studios and the 'independents'. Independent US film producers tend to be minor players in the international market compared with the Hollywood majors. But the majors – Paramount Pictures, Universal, 20th Century Fox, Warner Brothers, Disney, Metro Goldwyn Mayer and Sony/Columbia Pictures – are large, well-resourced and vertically integrated film distribution companies. The films produced and distributed by these seven companies dominate international film markets across the globe year after year.

One of the main factors favouring the Hollywood-based majors is size. This is important, not only in terms of demand (i.e. the size of domestic US market available to support their output), but also in terms of supply (i.e. the scale of productive activity each of the majors is engaged in). Total expenditure on filmed entertainment (through the box-office, home video plus television) amounted to an estimated $39 billion in 1999 in the USA alone, and US-made films accounted for a 92 per cent share of domestic cinema admissions (Screen Digest, 2000c: 189). The $35 billion or more spent in the USA each year on consuming domestically made feature films provides very considerable resources to support new production of high-budget movies. The ability of the major studios to make sizeable 'slates' of high-budget well-promoted movies every year, as opposed to only being involved in one-off film projects, means that these companies are particularly well positioned to spread their risks and to sustain a high share of the market.

Structure is the other area where the US industry has a big advantage over the UK and other would-be rivals. The distinction between majors and independents is important here. The US majors consist of integrated film companies whose activities span both production and distribution. The major studios produce only around 140 films in-house between them each year, but typically it is these 140 films that gain top positions in international markets for feature films. Films distributed by the majors usually account for well over 90 per cent of takings at the US box-office and everywhere else their market share is usually above 50 per cent of total revenues.

The independent sector is made up of all film producers worldwide except the majors. It comprises 'those companies – both within the US and around the world – that develop, finance and distribute feature films independently of the US major studios' (Lewis and Marris, 1991: 4). In a few cases, independence from the majors is not absolute. A handful of the more successful independents are now backed by much larger parent corporations with cross-ownership interests in the Hollywood majors, e.g. New Line Cinema is owned by Time Warner and Miramax by Disney (Hart-Wilden, 1997: 14). Aside from these, there is a large international population of genuinely independent film-production companies. In the USA, for example, independents produce more than three times as many films as the Hollywood studios each year. However, fewer than half of the films made by independents in the USA manage to gain a theatrical release. Elsewhere in the world, independent film producers experience similar difficulties in gaining access to exhibition.

The main difference between the Hollywood major studios and independents is that the majors are all vertically integrated companies that incorporate both production and distribution. Distribution involves not only finding suitable exhibition outlets for a film but also the co-ordination of an appropriate marketing and publicity campaign to generate interest in it. The distribution divisions of the majors cover virtually all territories in the world and, crucially, this gives companies such as Fox and Warner Brothers control over domestic and international dissemination of their product. 'With control of distribution, the risks of film-making can be spread across a large number of films, and between production and distribution' (Lewis and Marris, 1991: 4). With assured distribution, the majors are able to commit significant resources both to production and to marketing or P&A (prints and advertising) so as to build audience awareness of their own product. Independent producers who lack such control over distribution are clearly at a disadvantage. They can only reduce the risks involved in production by separately pre-selling the distribution rights to several territories before a film is made.

In the so-called 'classic' film economy, vertically integrated companies – i.e. the Hollywood majors – provide the finance for film production and use their own distribution networks to disseminate their films onwards to exhibition outlets. They exhibit where possible in their own cinemas. A proportion of their profits is reinvested in new production so as to keep the virtuous circle going. Typically, the distribution division (which is responsible for sales and marketing) will have an important say in which projects are pursued and which are not, so that production is strongly influenced by marketing considerations right from the outset. The general success of this model stems from two main factors: control over distribution plus the ability to produce a steady outflow of films. This ensures that income from the few hits or blockbusters produced by each of the majors each year is available to cover whatever losses are incurred by the flops and the average performers.

VERTICAL STRUCTURE AND RISK-SPREADING

Like fashion and popular music, film production is a hit-or-miss business. It is not only risky but also highly expensive. Average production budgets for a major Hollywood movie were running at some $51 million in 1999 (Andrews, 2000: 1) plus an additional 50 per cent or so for P&A. Production budgets are subject to fairly constant upward pressure, mainly because of inflation in the fees that brand-name stars can command. The heavy investment and high risks involved in the film industry have led to it being likened to the oil-exploration sector. As Headland and Relph put it, '[a] great deal of money can be spent drilling wells that trickle rather than gush' (1991: 6).

Investment in production of feature films, wherever it is carried out, is regarded as highly speculative. Typically, only two out of every ten films made even by the most successful Hollywood studios make profits (Gasson, 1996: 184). In other words, the majority of films lose money. Typically, the scale of revenues created by hits at the box-office is enormous, even relative to the sizeable budgets which are necessary to create them in the first place. So for the Hollywood majors, revenues from just two successes out of every ten films provide the cash-flow needed to continue replenishing the stream of well-promoted big-budget Hollywood movies in between the hits, and to provide a return to shareholders. For independent producers, it is almost impossible to break into this virtuous cash-flow circle enjoyed by the majors.

All the finance needed to fund the development, production and market-ing of a film has to be raised in advance, but returns do not start to flow until after the completed film reaches the cinemas, which is often some three years later or more. If the producer is attached to one of the major studios, then the studio will organize production finance internally. But independent producers must seek finance through an advance from a distributor against future box-office revenues and through borrowing and investment by third parties. The latter is difficult to come by and expensive because all the working capital involved in the film represents 'risk capital' in that, apart from the film itself (which is not yet made), there are no assets against which borrowing can be secured.

When the film's release date arrives and theatrical revenues begin to flow, the cinema covers its own costs first. The cinema-owner takes a cut directly from the gross box-office receipts to cover the costs of running the venue. After deduction of these expenses, called the 'house nut', the remainder is divided between the exhibitor and the distributor. A 90:10 split in favour of the distributor is not unusual, but the exact terms on which net box-office receipts are shared between the cinema and the distributor vary according to the film, the duration of the theatrical run and other circumstances. The 'distributor's gross' goes back to the distributor, who deducts commission and costs, including all advertising and promotional costs. Anything left after this is then passed on to the equity investors or financiers who have covered production costs, and who deduct a premium for covering risks, etc. Finally, any profit remaining goes back to the producer and (if appropriate) the production studio.

So, generally speaking, the investor or financier (unless it happens to be a distributor) is second from last in the repayment chain from the film's proceeds, followed only by the producer. His or her place in the queue may be pushed back even further if some of the key people involved in producing the film decide to take a proportion of their fee in the form of a participation in gross revenues. Top film stars can jump to the front of the queue by negotiating a cut of the film's so-called 'first dollar' receipts – i.e. box-office receipts before deduction of any distribution costs. For example, Hollywood actor Jim Carrey is part of a group of highly sought after actors who are able to demand so-called '20/20 packages' – i.e. a $20 million up-front fee for participation plus 20 per cent of the film's 'first dollar' receipts (Parkes and Harding, 2000: 25).

Going back to the example of the oil industry, companies such as Shell, Esso and BP are normally involved in the whole cycle from exploration to refining to sales of petrol at the filling-station forecourt. Consequently, they can spread the costs of the riskiest element (drilling) across the return from the whole process. The Hollywood majors work on the same principle. They control production and distribution and, in many cases, are also involved in exhibition. In the UK, for example, several multiplex cinema sites are run by subsidiaries of the US majors. This means that, in the UK as in many other countries, not only are the majority of box-office revenues accounted for by Hollywood distributors and Hollywood product but the exhibitor's cut very frequently ends up in the pockets of the US majors rather than with domestic players (unless the cinema is part of the Odeon chain). So, as with the large oil companies, the expensive risk phase (i.e. production) is covered by total returns to the film company on each phase of the entire and ongoing process of supply to the consumer.

The accumulation of market power stretching across all phases in the vertical supply chain creates a number of important advantages for the US major studios. It ensures wide exhibition and therefore a dominant market position for the supply of their own products. Every film produced, even the failures, can be fed into the distribution business to achieve some earnings. Because of their control over the supply chain, major distributors can engage in trade practices such as 'block booking' – i.e. when exhibitors are required to take a bundle of films, including some they might not otherwise have wanted to exhibit – which help to reduce their risks (Hoskins et al., 1997: 55–6). Vertical integration also means that there are no (or fewer) third-party distributors or other middle-men taking a cut from the return to the original investor – i.e. the studios themselves.

THE UK PRODUCTION SECTOR

The success of US-made films in international markets has created concern about indigenous film-making in other countries. Across Europe, where domestic films generally account for a low and declining share of home markets, the dominance of the Hollywood majors has raised questions about the economic viability of indigenous film production and about the need for protective interventions. The UK situation exemplifies the main problems faced in other European countries even though, to some extent, the UK market is more open to US imports than countries that are not English-speaking. The basic economic problems for the UK production sector, like every other national film production industry in Europe, stem from its size and its structure.

Looking at the issue of size first, a national film industry depends on a strong home market where there is demand for its product and where most of its production costs can be covered. The UK market for film products has grown consistently since the mid-1980s and is currently worth around £3 billion per year. However, it is dominated overwhelmingly by Hollywood product. To some extent, this reflects a ready acceptance in the UK of imported films in the English language. But the pattern of US dominance seems to recur throughout Europe, even in countries that are perceived as resistant to US cultural imports, such as France (Table 6.2).

With a high level of US import penetration, UK and other national European film production sectors have become relatively small players in their own home markets. Consequently, they are also very minor players in international film markets. In contrast with the USA, the available home

TABLE 6.2   Share of cinema admissions for
US films, 1999 (%)

USA	92.1
UK	80.8
Germany	76.5
Spain	72.1
Italy	62.1
France	56.8

Source: Screen Digest and European Audiovisual
Observatory data cited in Screen Digest, 2000c:
189

market for UK films is not large enough to allow investors to meet all the production costs of a film and to expect to recover their investment on any consistent basis. So investment in UK film production is extremely risky. Local producers find themselves caught in a vicious circle: with few UK films achieving success at the box-office (successes such as *Four Weddings and a Funeral* and *The Full Monty* are exceptional), there is little incentive for distributors to put up the finance for films made by UK producers. UK film productions tend to have relatively small budgets, which works against them in terms of marketability.

Size is an important issue, not only in terms of the available home market but also in terms of the level of production being carried out. The UK production sector produces too few films every year to be a key player in international markets. In addition, the large number of different production companies involved in generating this output means that no UK player is large enough to effectively spread the risks of failure.

The number of titles produced in the UK (Table 6.3) averaged around 60 films per year throughout the 1980s and 1990s. A mini-boom in UK film production in the late 1990s is largely accounted for by the introduction in 1995 of public grants for film-makers from National Lottery proceeds. More generally, the scale of production activity in the UK is simply not enough to make any impact on international distribution. The entire slate of around 40–50 'wholly UK' films made each year is not sufficient to make the UK an important supplier in the world market for feature films. Indeed, many UK-made films are considered too small and

TABLE 6.3   Number and value of UK film productions, 1981–98

Year	Titles produced	Current prices (£m)	Production cost (£m) (1999 prices)
1981	24	61.2	134.8
1982	40	141.1	286.3
1983	51	251.1	487.4
1984	53	270.4	495.4
1985	54	269.4	469.4
1986	41	165.8	279.4
1987	55	195.3	315.3
1988	48	175.2	272.2
1989	30	104.7	149.7
1990	60	217.4	280.2
1991	59	243.2	294.1
1992	47	184.9	215.1
1993	67	224.1	260.7
1994	84	455.2	518.3
1995	78	402.4	454.7
1996	128	741.4	809.3
1997	116	562.8	599.9
1998	88	509.3	525.0

Source: Screen Finance/x25 Partnership/BFI cited in BFI, 2000: 19

uncommercial ever to make it to the cinema. A high and increasing proportion of UK-made films is left, literally, sitting on the shelf (BFI, 2000: 24).

Part of the explanation for this problem can found by analysing the average budget size of UK films and comparing it with those in the USA. At under £6 million per title in 1998, average production costs for UK-made films were well below the $50 million production budgets typical of US major feature films in the same year. The gap between UK and US budgets is substantially wider if marketing costs are taken into account. In 1997, the average P&A spend on a Hollywood film was in the region of $19 million compared with an average spend of £0.5 million per title to promote UK films (Hart-Wilden, 1997: 21). So, virtually all films made by the UK production sector are 'low budget' projects and they tend to be relatively under-promoted.

The fragmented structure of the UK industry is another major draw-back. No single film production company is churning out enough films to facilitate cross-subsidization and effective risk-spreading. In addition, the UK production, distribution and exhibition sectors are vertically disaggregated. The UK production sector makes films but is not directly involved in distribution nor in exhibition. Lack of integration of domestic production and distribution is a problem in very many other European countries also. This separation leaves domestic producers with very little leverage in their dealings with the big distribution chains.

Distribution in the UK, as across Europe, is dominated by the major Hollywood studios. In Europe, the distribution subsidiaries of three of the US majors – Paramount, Universal and Metro Goldwyn Mayer – joined forces in the mid-1990s under the auspices of United International Pictures (UIP). The remaining four – 20th Century Fox, Warner Brothers, Disney and Sony/Columbia Pictures – each handle distribution of their own product, Disney under the name of Buena Vista. Table 6.4 provides a breakdown of box-office receipts by distributor in 1998. It indicates that well over 80 per cent of the UK box office is accounted for by products distributed by the US majors.

Many of the majors handle US product almost exclusively and are reluctant to provide any production finance for local film-makers. But whether a stronger market share for domestic UK distributors would improve matters is a debatable question. All commercial distributors, whether or not they are subsidiaries of the US majors, are inclined to offer the best release dates and most attractive financial terms to whichever suppliers can be relied upon to provide profitable product – i.e. the Hollywood majors. Commercial exhibitors, in turn, have a natural preference for big-budget, well-promoted movies that can be relied on to attract large audiences – i.e. Hollywood movies. So, for the domestic

TABLE 6.4   UK box-office by distributor, 1998

Distributor	Titles	Box-office*
1 20th c Fox	17	129,562,323
2 UIP	36	119,378,163
3 Buena Vista	27	98,013,512
4 Warner	25	46,967,601
5 Columbia	15	32,750,941
Total US majors	120	426,672,540
1 Entertainment	22	45,404,914
2 PolyGram	22	25,421,233
3 Film Four	12	5,328,848
4 Pathé	16	3,196,645
5 First Independent	7	1,516,921
6 Artificial Eye	18	1,345,749
7 Alliance	11	1,044,382
8 Metrodome	8	910,578
9 Eros	6	820,277
10 Feature Film Co.	11	644,646
Others	76	2,426,592
Total (Independents)	209	88,060,785
Total	329	514,733,325

* UK and Ireland

Source: ACNielsen EDI/BFI/Screen Finance/x25 Partnership cited in BFI, 2000: 38

production sector, the problem is not so much lack of market presence in distribution as lack of vertically integrated corporate structures that enable close links to be forged between these interdependent functions.

In summary, the small size of the domestic UK market and the dis-aggregated structure of the industry prevent the indigenous production sector from growing beyond a cottage industry. Exactly the same problems are evident in other European countries and, indeed, the European market as a whole remains 'almost completely fragmented' (Screen Digest, 2000c: 189). The domination of the US majors both in the UK and across European film product markets appears to be self-perpetuating and, to the concern of European policy-makers, has gradually strengthened over time.

OBSTACLES TO INVESTMENT IN 'INDEPENDENT' PRODUCTION

The distribution power of the US majors affects all independent film-makers so the majority, irrespective of nationality, find it difficult to attract third-party investment (i.e. from parties other than distributors) for their projects. A study carried out on behalf of the Department of National Heritage in the UK in 1996 identified three barriers to the growth of the UK film production sector – the structure of the industry, financial obstacles and communication problems (Middleton, 1996: 3). These impediments are typical of the problems encountered by independent producers when they seek commercial investment backing for film projects.

According to the Middleton Report, the fundamental difficulty is that the structure of independent production is too fragmented. The sector is comprised of too many small companies that are under-capitalized and unable to spread risk across a slate of films. Very few UK production companies are large enough to make more than one film per year (Hart-Wilden, 1997: 12). In addition, they tend to raise money for their productions on a film-by-film basis. This small scale approach 'allows for no cross-collateralisation between successful and unsuccessful projects' (Middleton, 1996: 12). There are no opportunities for investors in UK film production to offset losses on some investments against gains made elsewhere.

Another obvious impediment is that both distribution and exhibition are dominated by the US majors. Independent producers are in a very weak negotiating position with distributors and most do not have sufficient market power to ensure good distribution. Potential investors are naturally deterred by the lack of certainty surrounding what level of distribution access a film will achieve.

So the risk:reward ratio associated with investment in film production is generally seen by financiers as unfavourable (Middleton, 1996: 4). Risks are too high and rewards, although potentially high, are too uncertain. Supporting individual films is not a particularly attractive proposition. But since independent production companies are generally unable to build up the stable and successful track record needed to attract investment in the firm, no suitable vehicle for investment can be presented to the financial community. In addition, according to Middleton, there is not enough communication between film-makers and professional financiers to alter the perception that films are simply a 'no go' area (1996: 14).

However, no matter how much improvement were to be achieved in communication between the worlds of film and finance, the structural deficiencies that afflict the sector would remain at the heart of its problems. In the independent sector, the process of making and supplying films is broken into a number of isolated stages and the cost of the riskiest element (production) is normally borne by the financier of that phase only. As we saw earlier, the position of third-party investors in the repayment chain from a film's profits is far from favourable and, in any event, most independent films fail to cover their costs. So, independent film producers often find themselves in a relentless cycle of low investment and limited commercial success.

Apart from major film distributors and third-party financiers or investors, another possible source of finance for independent film producers
may be the television industry. Feature films occupy an important position
in the schedules of many broadcasters. In the UK, some television
companies are prepared to invest regularly in low-budget domestic films
and Channel Four, for example, has done so with a degree of success.
But even television companies are liable to be put off by the prevailing
market structure which is so disadvantageous to all product other than
that supplied by the US majors. Broadcasters need films but it is far less
risky and less costly to acquire the television rights for a second-hand
Hollywood film than it is to invest in new production.

Any potential investor, unless it also happens to be a distributor, will
naturally be concerned about the prospects for an independent film during
the distribution stage. The preference for market-driven Hollywood films
as opposed to what Hoskins et al. (1997: 65) describe as 'high-culture'
independent production is extremely widespread amongst distributors and
it reflects what are perceived to be the demands and preferences of the
majority of cinema-goers. Low-budget and relatively under-promoted
independent films – which includes most European features – are, on the
whole, avoided by exhibitors as non-commercial products unlikely to
attract a large following.

The obstacles that stand between independent film producers and
sources of production finance are high but not insurmountable. Some have
suggested that, in order to improve their financial circumstances,
independent producers in the UK and across Europe ought to emulate
the more market-driven approach which has brought such success to the
US majors. Perhaps this is so but, even with projects that have great
commercial appeal, independents still find it difficult to compete against
the built-in advantages of size and structure of the Hollywood majors.
As things stand, it is difficult to see how the strength of the majors' grip
on international distribution can be challenged. Independent producers
cannot themselves expect to gain any foothold in distribution unless
they make films that many people will want to watch. Yet, whenever an
independent producer achieves a commercial hit, it is generally the
distribution arm of a major Hollywood studio that reaps the majority of
financial benefits.

IMPACT OF NEW TECHNOLOGIES

The introduction of digital technologies has encouraged hope among some
independents that the supply chain for film might be revolutionized. Digital

technology is affecting both production and distribution. In production, the use of digital cameras, editing and other equipment has greatly reduced the capital and labour costs potentially involved in making feature-length productions. A number of producers in the late 1990s, such as Danish film-makers Dogme, demonstrated the commercial viability of using low-cost digital production techniques. The vast majority of feature film producers continue to use celluloid but the opportunity to create film more cheaply using digital technology has reduced entry barriers to the production sector and provides independents with 'a cheaper way . . . to hone their craft' (Drinnan, 2000: 3).

The effect of digital techniques on production costs is not entirely deflationary. Digital manipulation and computer graphics can reduce the costs of capturing spectacular special effects but, on the other hand, some digital epics such as the second episode of the new *Star Wars* trilogy which began shooting in 2000 have involved exceptionally high production costs (Andrews, 2000: 1). Even so, digitization is opening up opportunities for small independent film-makers. The success of ultra-low-budget feature *The Blair Witch Project* in 1999 showed how digital technologies provide cheap and innovative ways not only to produce but also to promote films. The producers of *Blair Witch* were highly successful in using chat-sites and word-of-mouth across the Internet to create hype and draw attention to the movie long before film critics had access to it.

Digital technology is also affecting the ways in which film is distributed. Times have changed considerably since the early 1980s when the cinema box-office was by far and away the most important source of revenue for film-makers. By 1999, theatrical income represented only 26 per cent of the combined US and international film revenues for the US majors (Screen Finance: 2000). Television and, especially, video revenues are now much more significant. But digital technology is expected to make television an even more central avenue to the consumer in future.

A steady increase in the proportion of US and international film revenues accounted for by television throughout the 1990s reflects growth in the number and popularity of subscription movie channels throughout the period (for UK figures see Table 6.1 on p. 104). Since the late 1990s, the extra channel capacity made possible by digital compression techniques has facilitated the development of additional film services on television where, to a greater or lesser extent, viewers are empowered to select which titles they want to watch. Personalized film services such as pay-per-view (where viewers can choose between, perhaps, four or five recent titles at fixed transmission times) or 'near video-on-demand' (involving a choice of more alternatives, with staggered starting times) allow for much higher individual charges to be levied from television viewers than in the past.

Following on from pay-per-view and near video-on-demand (NVOD), the next category of movie service on the horizon is real video-on-demand (VOD). VOD services, for which new pilot projects were initiated both in the UK and Germany in 2000, will enable viewers to choose from a wide catalogue of titles and to download films at any time of the day or night in return for a fee (Clark, 2000: 40). The main selling points for viewers are 'choice, convenience and control' (Davies, 2000: 7). VOD removes such problems as video-shop closing times and damaged second-hand cassettes. Its advantages have led many to predict that so-called 'cyber-video stores will one day overtake their rivals – the tens of thousands of musty video stores on Europe's high streets' (Clark, 2000: 37).

However, the technical costs associated with VOD are still high and, as with other interactive television services, it requires considerable net-work capacity (Davies, 2000: 7). Its success depends on how speedily cable and telecommunications infrastructures are developed and upgraded. Television delivery of VOD could, of course, be overtaken by similar services on the Internet with subscribers downloading film choices directly to their PCs in return for a payment.

The idea that the Internet could revolutionize distribution of film is one that several independent film-makers have warmed to. According to the writer-director of hit morality comedy *Jerry Maguire*, the Internet should level the playing field for films when seeking theatrical access: 'In terms of gaining attention for movies, it equalises everything' (Crowe cited in Andrews, 2000:1). The *Blair Witch* example showed how useful the Internet can be in targeting potential film-goers and creating awareness of a film. To the extent that other independent producers manage to utilize this tool effectively, the control that distributors currently exert over flows of information to the consumer about forthcoming films might be challenged. Independent films that succeed in acquiring a 'must see' status are naturally going to be attractive to exhibitors, irrespective of whether or not they are backed by major distributors.

The Internet can also be used as a direct gateway between independent producers and audiences for their work, thus (arguably) altogether by-passing the need for conventional distributors and exhibitors. A distribution system based on millions of negotiations between individual producers and consumers carried out over the Internet is feasible, at least in theory. But, in reality, doubts exist about whether most audiences would want to watch entire feature-length films on their PCs (Pickard, 2000: 6; Vickers, 2000: 55). Moreover, the roles played by conventional distributors in reducing transaction costs, providing production finance and sustaining very high levels of consumer expenditure on film throughout successive release windows bring important benefits to the film industry as a whole.

One area where digital technology could cut down on distribution costs is on delivery of film to cinemas. The use of blanket exhibition strategies by major distributors means that many physical copies of the celluloid prints of a film have to be created and transported to cinemas on time for the film's launch date. Each print is expensive to make and the need to physically reproduce prints would be eliminated if they were delivered electronically instead. However, electronic delivery can only work if exhibitors have digital screening equipment and, at present, few have invested in such technology.

Whether the introduction of digital methods of delivery would fundamentally alter which sorts of films gain access to cinemas is highly questionable (Drinnan, 2000: 3). The dominance of the US majors in distribution is based not so much on efficiency in delivering physical product to exhibitors worldwide but on their ability to supply exhibitors with a constant flow of product that is well promoted and attractive to audiences. So long as the majors retain this ability, advances in production or distribution technologies are unlikely to destabilize their position.

seven

PRINT MEDIA

This chapter focuses on the economics of newspaper and magazine publishing. It introduces the distinctive revenue, cost and market characteristics of print media, highlighting the impact of recent advances in publishing and print technologies. Concepts of consumer surplus, market segmentation and internationalization are examined in the context of the business strategies deployed by print media organizations. The use of aggressive pricing strategies is examined, drawing on relevant empirical examples from the newspaper industry, as are the key factors involved in determining an optimal pricing strategy.

After studying this chapter, you should be able to:

- Understand the economic characteristics associated with print media
- Explain the sorts of competitive tools available to print media operators
- Analyse the issues involved in determining a newspaper's optimal pricing strategy
- Assess which factors have encouraged the success of transnational magazine publishing in Europe
- Explain why strategies of segmentation of demand are important in magazine publishing

CHARACTERISTICS OF NEWSPAPER PUBLISHING

Newspapers are the original 'mass' medium. Newspaper publishing gained importance as an economic activity during the latter half of the nineteenth century when improvements in printing technology and the spread of literacy made possible the introduction of newspaper titles with very large or mass circulations. The industry flourished during the 1920s and 1930s in the UK, across Europe and in the USA. The arrival of commercial television in the 1950s, however, marked the beginning of a period of gradual decline for newspaper publishing and, since then, many firms in the industry have been forced to adjust to increasingly difficult market conditions.

Newspapers participate in what was referred to earlier as a 'dual-product' market. Newspaper content (news reports, features, etc.) is produced by journalists and editors in order to attract readers. Access to readers is then priced and sold to advertisers (Picard, 1998: 116-17). Some newspapers rely on advertising income alone to cover their costs and earn profits. For example, the *Metro* newspaper titles originally launched by Swedish group MTG in 1995 are dailies which are given away free to commuters 'from Stockholm to Santiago' and they make money solely from the sale of advertising space (Brown-Humes, 2000: 35). But the vast majority of newspaper titles are supported by a combination of revenue from copy sales and from advertising.

The overall quantity and the demographic profile of a newspaper's readers (i.e. the proportion of its readers that fit into different social and income classifications) are key determinants of its income. In the UK, cover sales income generally provides around half of all newspaper revenues and the remainder comes from the sale of advertising space. The breakdown between advertising and sales income varies from one title to the next, depending on market position and readership. The UK national newspaper market can be subdivided into at least two broad segments: up-market or 'quality' titles and mass-market or 'popular' titles. As shown in Figure 7.1, so-called quality newspapers aimed at wealthier socio-economic sections of the population tend to derive a higher proportion of their income from advertising than their more popular tabloid rivals.

It is notable from newspaper consumption patterns that the more affluent sectors of society read slightly more newspapers than the less well off (Wedell and Luyken, 1986; Ostergaard, 1992). This pattern tends to exist internationally, even though newspapers are often given preferential direct tax treatment to encourage wider sales to lower income groups. In the UK, no VAT is charged on newspapers, which effectively provides a form of public subsidy to newspaper readers. Many other European countries apply discounted and preferential VAT rates to sales of newspapers, books and other products that convey 'knowledge'.

The prevalent pattern of higher newspaper consumption amongst more affluent sections of the population reflects both supply- and demand-side

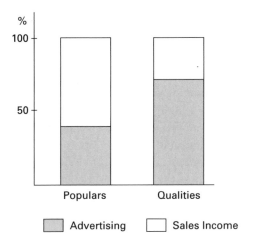

FIGURE 7.1   National UK dailies: sources of revenue in 1999 (data from Advertising Association, 2000: 23)

factors. Higher demand for newspapers and magazines amongst those who are better-off may be accounted for by lifestyle and educational issues. On the supply-side, competition between publishers to provide those readership profiles which are most attractive to advertisers results in a higher proportion of print media products aimed at groups of individuals that earn high incomes. In the UK, for example, a breakdown of national newspaper readership patterns by socio-economic class indicates that As and Bs, who account for about 21 per cent of the national population, have more titles aimed at them than C2s and DEs, who accounted for over 50 per cent of the population in 1998 (Advertising Association, 1999: 98).[1]

This is not to suggest that newspapers overlook less affluent segments of the population. On the contrary, even without any industry regulator forcing it to serve all segments of the public, the UK national newspaper industry has tended to be much more efficient than terrestrial television at supplying a diverse range of output aimed at different interest groups (Hughes and Vines, 1989: 44). This diversity is possible because the UK national newspaper market is large enough to support several titles and because newspapers are supported by a direct charge as well as by advertising. Whereas advertising-supported television channels (especially when there are only a few) will tend to compete head-on with one another for

---

1. The classification system widely used by advertisers in the UK involves five broad socio-economic categories: A (Upper Professional); B (Lower Professional); C1 (Clerical); C2 (Skilled Manual); D (Unskilled); E (Unemployed).

the same mainstream mass audience, the direct charge for newspapers makes it economically feasible for individual titles to concentrate on serving particular segments of the market.

Provided that any newspaper market is sufficiently large and affluent then, in theory, it is possible that several titles can operate profitably by serving different segments of the whole spectrum of consumer interest. Newspapers that reach a high proportion of As and Bs will, of course, be able to attract a premium in the advertising rates they charge. For example, the cost per thousand (readers) rate for a UK quality title such as the *Daily Telegraph* is typically at least two or three times higher than for a 'popular' title such as the *Mirror* or the *Sun* (Sparks, 1999: 52). A title may seek to maximize revenues by, for example, targeting small but affluent readership segments (as does the *Financial Times*) or by pursuing mass circulations of less affluent readers (as does the *Sun*). Figure 7.2 indicates the very significant differential between the levels of net revenue per copy that popular and quality daily UK titles earned in 1999, in terms both of sales income and, especially, advertising.

As discussed in Chapter 3, advertising can be subdivided into display and classified, the latter referring to recruitment, housing and personal advertisements. Classified advertising is an important source of income for newspapers, especially regional newspapers. This category is less vulnerable to competition from broadcast media than is display advertising. On the other hand, classified advertising is highly sensitive to cyclical upturns and downturns and, in recession, tends to fall further

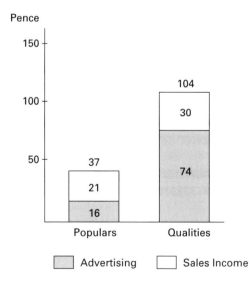

FIGURE 7.2   National UK dailies: publishers' net revenue per copy sold, 1999
(data from Advertising Association, 2000: 13)

and faster than display advertising as employment, housing and car sales markets stagnate. In addition, the Internet is perceived as 'a very good vehicle for classified advertising' so the development of the Internet poses a potential threat to newspaper industry revenues over the medium and longer term (Zenith Media, 2001: 117).

As with other media sectors, the newspaper industry is characterized by relatively high initial or 'first copy' costs and low marginal costs (Picard, 1998: 121–2). The fixed costs – editorial, administration, etc. – involved in newspaper publishing are high, and variable costs – e.g. newsprint – are relatively low. Hence, the industry is characterized by economies of scale. Even so, production of newspapers does involve some marginal costs. The main source of value for readers may be the stories, news and ideas conveyed in their daily newspaper but they also require the physical medium on which these messages are conveyed.

The physical production and printing of newspapers is one area where costs have reduced dramatically since the early 1980s. Up until then, each page had to be typeset manually and newspapers were dependent on highly skilled and (in the UK) heavily unionized workforces to keep their printing presses running. The arrival of new computer technology that allowed newspaper pages to be made up electronically suddenly meant that large numbers of typesetters were no longer required to carry out this task. In the UK, the introduction of new technology was fiercely resisted by the powerful print unions until the country's largest newspaper publisher, News International, finally managed to introduce it at new production sites for its four national titles at Wapping in 1985.

Changes in UK labour laws in the early 1980s that restricted the power of trade unions were instrumental in allowing Rupert Murdoch's News International to finally quash resistance to the introduction of new labour-saving production technologies. The replacement of the old hot metal printing presses with modern cold metal technology and on-screen page make-up software meant that extensive labour costs could be eliminated. Other UK newspaper publishers who had 'acquiesced for years to out-rageous manning levels and demands for special payments to avoid disruption and loss of revenue' were quick to seize the opportunity created by Murdoch's success in the Wapping dispute to drive through their own 'voluntary' deals with the unions (Snoddy, 1996: 23). Thousands of jobs were lost in the late 1980s as one newspaper group after another switched over to the latest technology at new printing plants, mostly located in the London docklands.

The move to electronic typesetting and modern printing technology in the 1980s required very significant capital investment but it resulted in greatly improved operating margins for newspaper publishers in the UK and elsewhere across Europe and in the USA. Valuable gains were made in terms of reducing the fixed production costs involved in creating the 'first copy' of a newspaper. However, variable manufacturing costs are still a feature of newspaper publishing. Once the printing presses are running, the cost of paper and ink have to be considered. Paper or newsprint typically accounts for some 20 per cent of a newspaper's total costs (Gasson, 1996: 74).

Newsprint prices are notoriously volatile, depending on world supply and demand for paper. The cost of newsprint jumped by around 50 per cent between 1993 and 1995 before settling back down again in the late 1990s. It is expected to increase again by at least 10–20 per cent across Europe in 2001 (George, 2001: 16). Newspaper publishers may, to some extent, be able to respond to sudden price increases by cutting usage – for example by lowering pagination, reducing the width of their pages or even moving to a tabloid format. But there is a limit to how far the industry can protect itself against cyclical ups and downs in the cost of this basic raw material.

Newspaper publishing involves some marginal newsprint and printing costs. Distribution is another cost that has variable components, depending on the overall volume of newspapers involved. Publishers in the UK rely on a network of wholesalers and retailers, each of whom takes a cut of the cover price, to ensure that their product is distributed to newsagents and paper-stands across the country. Arrangements tend to differ in regional newspaper markets and, in some cases, newspaper publishers themselves are vertically integrated into the downstream activity of distribution.

Editorial and administrative overheads are the largest component of a newspaper publisher's costs (Gasson, 1996: 74). These are relatively fixed, irrespective of a newspaper's circulation figures. As discussed in Chapter 2, economies of scope may arise for newspaper proprietors that publish more than one title. Publishers of several titles may be able to combine back-office activities, such as administration, finance and personnel. Some, though not all, publishers encourage sharing of editorial output between different titles where material relevant to more than one paper has been gathered. The centralization of advertising sales can also produce worthwhile cost-efficiencies for multi-product newspaper publishers.

The relationship between a newspaper title's operating costs and the levels of audience or readership it can attract is not necessarily a clearly defined and linear one. The decision about where (editorially, politically, etc.) a newspaper positions itself in the market is a key determinant of its potential circulation and, thus, its income. But there is no particular reason why the overheads (editorial, printing, distribution, etc.) involved in serving one segment of the population rather than another should differ significantly. In addition, because most newspaper costs are fixed, the opportunity to make savings if and when circulation falls is relatively limited (Picard, 1998: 122–3). This de-linkage between costs and revenues means that newspaper publishers, like broadcasters, are prone to vicious and virtuous circles of profitability. For example, a newspaper title that responds to a decline in circulation by paring back on dedicated journalistic staff and relying more heavily on news agencies as an inexpensive source of stories will run the risk of further declines in readership and more losses in sales and advertising income (Greenslade, 2001: 4-5).

The dominance of national newspapers in the UK is something of a peculiarity. In most large European countries other than the UK (e.g. France, Germany) and in the USA, regional dailies play a much more important role than national titles. Modernization and urbanization have created more demand for local communication and the structure of the press has evolved as a collection of small regional or city-based markets, providing mainly 'responsible' product (Wedell and Luyken, 1986). By contrast, there is predominant consumption of national rather than regional papers in Ireland, Australia and Japan.

The extent of competitiveness between newspapers depends on the size and wealth of the particular geographic market they are operating in and on the number of rival newspapers the market in question is able to support. Local or regional papers often operate in a monopoly situation because aggregate demand in a small market can only support one profitable title. At the same time, newspapers that operate as local monopolies are aware that their markets are potentially 'contestable' i.e. that a rival title may be launched on their patch. According to Snoddy (1993), newspapers that operate as local monopolies are forced by circumstances to serve all segments of the community and tend to display a certain 'respectability'. Larger markets (such as the UK national daily newspaper market), on the other hand, are more lucrative and much more ruthlessly competitive and this is reflected in a tendency towards more aggressively competitive and sensationalist products.

Newspaper publishers everywhere are generally faced with low growth prospects and with a gradual double-squeeze on their revenues. Historic trends in advertising in the UK as elsewhere show that, since the arrival of commercial television, there has been a slow but steady decline in newspapers' share of total advertising expenditure (Advertising Association, 2000: 38). Aggregate levels of newspaper sales and readership are also in long-term decline, especially at the popular end of the market (Sparks, 1999: 55). Publishers have responded to these trends in a number of ways. In the regional sector of the UK newspaper industry, ownership has become increasingly consolidated. In the national sector of the UK newspaper industry, competition for market share has intensified dramatically since the early 1990s.

USING COMPETITIVE STRATEGIES TO BUILD MARKET SHARE

The desire for a greater market share in the newspaper industry can readily be accounted for by long-term pressure on revenues in this sector. But tendencies towards concentration of press ownership have been in evidence since as early as the eighteenth century. Concentrated ownership patterns sometimes reflect motives other than profit maximization – for example a desire on the part of proprietors to gain political influence through ownership of a large number of newspaper titles. Yet oligopolistic tendencies in the newspaper industry also undoubtedly reflect the economic characteristics of the sector. The widespread availability of economies of scale in publishing means that, all other things being equal, the industry will naturally gravitate towards oligopoly and monopoly market structures.

A variety of strategies may be deployed in order to increase market share. Acquiring rival titles that are already well established is one option, so long as this is not prohibited by media and cross-media ownership restrictions. Launching new titles is another possibility. The launch of a new title by an incumbent may, by increasing the degree of perceived product differentiation in the market, serve to deter market entry by newcomers from outside the industry. As a result of changes in printing technology introduced in the 1970s and 1980s, the option of launching a new title is now more economically feasible. Even so, the high risks and heavy launch costs associated with establishing a new newspaper title will deter most from taking on such a strategy.

In terms of building market share for existing titles, product and price changes are the most important competitive tools at the publisher's disposal, although advertising and promotional activities may also be useful. Newspaper promotions such as competitions, special offers and discounts in return for tokens collected do tend to influence newspaper circulation and are a commonplace feature in newspaper markets. The main problem with promotional drives is that their impact on circulation generally tends to be short-lived.

Turning to the product itself, each title's unique selling point is the character of its news coverage or editorial content. It has occasionally been suggested that, in order for newspapers to survive, editors ought to become 'marketeers', seeking at all times to appeal to the widest number of readers by consulting with them regularly and adjusting their journalistic content in direct response to reader preferences. Successful long-established newspapers such as the *Telegraph* naturally do adjust their contents over time to reflect the social values of their readership, but they do so very gradually so as to maintain a strong identity and a loyal following. Newspapers that make sudden adjustments in the tone of their editorial coverage in order to court a wider readership run the risk of diluting or confusing their brand identity. So, the use of changes of content to boost readership and advertising is a tactic which has to be deployed with great subtlety if it is to be effective.

Changing the design or layout of a newspaper and introducing separate sections and supplements have all been used as competitive tools in order to improve a newspaper's marketability. Extra supplements were popular amongst UK titles in 1989–93 period, although the costs of additional pagination were acutely felt by newspaper publishers during the subsequent cyclical upswing in newsprint prices in the mid-1990s.

Another very important competitive tool is price: '[p]rices may be reduced in order to raise market share or else to defend existing market share in the face of greater competition' (Griffiths and Wall, 1999: 184). Price is the primary mode of competition in most consumer product markets but, in the newspaper industry, it is sometimes assumed that brand loyalty to particular titles is so strong that it would prevent changes in cover price from working as an effective competitive tool. The price war instigated by News International in the UK daily newspaper sector in 1993 has proven this viewpoint to be incorrect. Notwithstanding brand loyalty or even party-political allegiances that encourage newspaper readers to habitually purchase the same title, it appears that price also plays a strong part in sales patterns for newspapers.

How is the price of a newspaper set? In theory, a range of factors have a bearing on how any firm decides to price its products, including what sort of market structure it is operating in and what its objectives are. Assuming the firm seeks to maximize profits then costs will usually play a role in price determination. Cost-plus pricing is the practice whereby a price is arrived at by adding some percentage mark-up to the cost of producing a good. The extent to which prices charged exceed production costs may depend on how competitive the market structure is. A monopolist can get away with charging very high prices whereas the existence of rival suppliers in the market will encourage firms to compete by setting prices that are closer to costs, thus narrowing their own profit margins.

If the firm's main objective is something other than profit maximization then alternative principles will guide its pricing strategies. In the UK, some newspapers are clearly not run as profit-maximizing enterprises. For example, Guardian Newspaper Limited, which publishes both the *Guardian* and the *Observer*, is wholly owned by the Scott Trust, whose purpose is to protect the editorial independence and the continuation of its newspaper titles rather than to make profits from them. Other proprietors are generally less explicit about their motives but it is notable that several other well-established UK daily newspapers (including *The Times*) are sustained by their owners even though they do not make profits. When objectives other than profit maximization are present, production costs are not necessarily reflected in pricing decisions.

Market structure is a crucial factor governing price determination. A firm's pricing decision will depend on how many rival products are available, how similar these products are to its own and what pricing strategies rivals are engaged in. In perfectly competitive markets with many suppliers and buyers of products that are more or less the same (or homogeneous), all firms will be 'price-takers' – i.e. no firm will have sufficient market power to charge a higher price for its product than anyone else and all firms must set their price at the prevailing market rate. However, in oligopolistic markets, products tend to be somewhat differentiated. Consequently, each individual supplier has a certain degree of market power (including power to set prices) but so do all of its rivals.

The UK national newspaper industry operates in an oligopoly market structure. Price-setting under conditions of oligopoly is an uncertain business. Each firm tries to anticipate its rivals' reactions to its own pricing decision. Firms have to decide whether it is more advantageous to compete or to co-operate on pricing. Since explicit collusive behaviour is frowned upon by competition authorities, any co-operation between oligopolists may well be tacit rather than overt. Each of the firms in an oligopolistic industry, recognizing that all of them will make more profits as a group if they do not compete against each other through price-cutting, may tacitly arrive at an agreement to set prices within a given range.

Such informal agreements allow oligopolists to co-exist very comfortably. However, they also pose a dilemma. Firms may well have a common interest in finding and maintaining a 'co-operative equilibrium'. But it will usually pay any one of them to break ranks and cut its own price, so long as others do not do the same. Each firm in an oligopolistic market is naturally primarily interested in its own performance and any one of them can increase their profits, at least in the short term, by behaving in a rivalrous fashion. Of course, if other firms follow suit and reduce their prices too, then clearly the group as a whole will be worse off. Indeed, intense price competition – of the sort which was in evidence on and off throughout the 1990s in the national UK newspaper market – tends to produce an equilibrium in which firms are not even covering their full costs.

Competition for market share in the newspaper industry is liable to upset any tacit agreement to hold prices within a given range. Unilateral price cuts and competitive pricing strategies will be attractive so long as firms believe that there is a limit to the price consumers are willing to pay for one newspaper title in preference to another. For a newspaper firm trying to set its price, it is not enough simply to know whether circulation will rise or fall in response to any change in price. The questions is, by how much? To measure the responsiveness of demand to changes in price, economists use the concept of 'elasticity'.

The **price elasticity of demand** for a newspaper describes how sensitive or responsive its total circulation is to any change in its cover price. Price elasticity of demand varies from one newspaper title to another and for the same title within different price ranges. If demand for a newspaper is very elastic, it means that its total circulation is highly responsive to any price change. Demand which is 'inelastic' implies that changes in price will have relatively little impact on sales.

The main determinant of elasticity is the availability of substitutes or of products that are perceived as substitutes (Lipsey and Chrystal, 1995: 93). Naturally, all newspaper titles regard themselves as having distinctive voices and identities that give them a unique brand appeal. Newspapers are clearly *not* homogeneous products. They can be differentiated from each other by editorial character but most do not have impenetrable monopolies over segments of the consumer market. There is plenty of empirical evidence to suggest that degrees of brand loyalty vary from one newspaper title to the next and, in some cases, readers will switch their purchasing habits purely in response to price changes. Variations in the extent to which individual newspaper titles are perceived as acceptable substitutes for each other explain why demand for some titles tends to be more elastic than for others.

A high consumer surplus will make demand less price elastic. As discussed earlier, the concept of consumer surplus refers to the difference between what consumers would be willing to pay for a product and what they actually have to pay in terms of current market price. For some newspaper titles, the difference between market price and the maximum price that some of its readers would be prepared to pay to obtain that particular title will be high because, for instance, the sort of news content and analysis the paper provides is considered unique and is highly valued by readers. A newspaper such as the *Financial Times*, because of its specialist coverage of financial and business news that is not replicated to the same extent in any other UK daily title, is likely to generate a much higher consumers' surplus than titles whose content or editorial focus are not perceived as unique. The higher the extra valuation placed on each title over and above its market price, the slower its readers will be to switch purchasing habits in response to relative price changes.

The key concern in setting or changing the price for a newspaper is the likely impact on circulation. To calculate price elasticity of demand, data about circulation levels both before and after a price change is required. Price elasticity of demand for a newspaper can be measured as the ratio of the percentage change in circulation divided by the percentage change in cover price that brought it about. Using the Greek letter delta (Δ) to symbolize 'change in', a formula for price elasticity can be expressed as follows:

$$\text{Price elasticity of demand} = \frac{\%\ \Delta\ \text{circulation}}{\%\ \Delta\ \text{price}}$$

For example, a 20 per cent increase in circulation in response to a 10 per cent reduction in price implies a price elasticity of 2. In this example, because the price change instigates a larger percentage change in circulation (i.e. price elasticity of demand > 1), demand is said to be 'elastic'. In theory, demand can also be 'perfectly inelastic' (i.e. = 0) if a change in price brings no change in circulation, or 'inelastic' (i.e. < 1) if a percentage change in circulation is less than the percentage change in price, or 'unitary' (i.e. =1) if a price change brings about exactly the same percentage change in circulation. Price elasticity affects the sales revenue a newspaper will get if it changes its price. If, for example, demand is inelastic then total sales revenue will move in the same direction as any price change whereas if demand is elastic then total sales revenue will move in the opposite direction.

Economies of scale in the newspaper industry are such that marginal changes in circulation have relatively little impact on costs. So, the majority of costs being relatively fixed, profitability depends on maximizing total revenue. Revenues are earned not only from copy sales but also from advertising. In order to set a price that will maximize revenue, account must be taken of the knock-on effects of any changes on advertising income. Even when demand is known to be relatively inelastic (i.e. an increase in cover price would boost sales income), the publisher may avoid raising its price because the negative impact on circulation and, in turn, on advertising exceeds the gains available from higher sales revenue.

In other words, the objective of maximizing total income means that the price is lower than if the publisher were trying to maximize sales income alone. The desire to achieve high circulations to sell to advertisers acts as a constraint on cover prices for newspapers. Figure 7.2 on p. 122 demonstrates the full extent to which newspapers – especially at the quality end of the market – derive their income from advertising. An optimal newspaper pricing strategy must take this into account and strike the most profitable balance between copy sales income and advertising revenue.

In oligopolistic markets, where only a few firms dominate, a price-cutting strategy embarked upon by one firm is very likely to be followed by others. Price competition erodes the collective profits of industry participants, although individual firms may make gains. Economic theory suggests that, after short periods of price warfare, oligopoly markets are likely to settle down once again into prolonged periods of price stability (Griffiths and Wall, 1999: 121). In periods of price stability, 'non-price' competition is usually more intense and weapons such as packaging, promotions and advertising will be used by firms seeking to defend their market share.

PRICE WAR IN THE 'QUALITY' SEGMENT OF THE UK NEWSPAPER INDUSTRY

The quality segment of the UK national market provides an interesting case study of price warfare in the newspaper industry. This segment is composed of five broadsheet titles: *The Times, Daily Telegraph, Guardian, Independent* and *Financial Times*. Following a prolonged period of price stability in this market, in which all titles (other than the *Financial Times* which occupies a special niche in the market) set prices within a relatively close range, one title suddenly embarked on a price-cutting strategy in September 1993. Rupert Murdoch's News International reduced the cover price of *The Times* from 45p to 30p. Since then, a campaign of aggressive price reductions by *The Times* has increased its average daily circulation from 354,000 in August 1993 to around 723,000 as at February 2001.

The way in which the circulation of *The Times* has responded to price reduction conforms with the general rule that demand tends to be more elastic in the longer term than in the short term (Parkin et al., 1997: 104-5). Table 7.1 provides a series of historic price and circulation figures for *The Times*, starting just ahead of its initial price reduction in autumn 1993. Using this historic data, price elasticity of demand for *The Times* can be calculated over progressively longer periods of time.[2] The picture

TABLE 7.1   Price and circulation for *'The Times'*

	Price	Circulation
June 1993	45p	360,000
June 1994	20p	530,000
June 1995	20p	685,000
June 1996	26p*	730,000
June 1998	26p*	770,000
June 2000	30p	724,000

* Monday edition 10p, Tuesday–Friday 30p
Source: Audit Bureau of Circulation

2. To avoid having two different values for the price elasticity of demand depending on whether a price movement is upwards or downwards, the formula

From June 1993

1 Year: $\dfrac{\% \; \Delta \; C/\text{ Average C}}{\% \; \Delta \; P/\text{ Average P}} = \dfrac{+38\%}{-77\%} = 0.50$ (inelastic)

2 Years: $\dfrac{\% \; \Delta \; C/\text{ Average C}}{\% \; \Delta \; P/\text{ Average P}} = \dfrac{+62\%}{-77\%} = 0.81$

3 Years: $\dfrac{\% \; \Delta \; C/\text{ Average C}}{\% \; \Delta \; P/\text{ Average P}} = \dfrac{+68\%}{-54\%} = 1.25$ (elastic)

7 Years: $\dfrac{\% \; \Delta \; C/\text{ Average C}}{\% \; \Delta \; P/\text{ Average P}} = \dfrac{+67\%}{-40\%} = 1.68$ (elastic)

C= Circulation; P = Price

FIGURE 7.3   Price elasticity of demand for 'The Times'

which emerges (see Figure 7.3) shows that circulation has gradually become more responsive to changes in price for *The Times*. The explanation of the tendency for demand to become more elastic over time is that consumers often need time to get used to price changes before switching their purchasing habits. Given sufficient time, consumers will eventually find and substitute goods which have become relatively cheap for those which have become relatively expensive.

Price elasticity of circulation demand for *The Times*, which was initially quite inelastic, has increased fairly steadily since it began discounting its cover price so that, by June 2000, sales income was well in excess of pre-price-war levels. Thus, News Corporation's initial losses can be seen as a successful strategic investment in building its share of the 'quality' segment of the UK market. *The Times* started out with a market share of 17 per cent of the collective circulation of *The Times*, *Daily Telegraph*, *Guardian* and *Independent* in August 1993 but this had increased to a 30 per cent market share by August 2000. As the price charged for *The Times* has gradually crept back up again, News International has recovered the losses it sustained during the early period of discounting. Higher circulation has not only brought in extra sales income but, crucially, has also narrowed the gap in readership levels between *The Times* and the current market leader, the *Daily Telegraph*. So, additional circulation has also increased the advertising revenue earned by *The Times*.

generally used to calculate it uses average price and average quantity (or, in this case, circulation) figures. So, for example, the change in the price of *The Times* between June 1993 and June 1994 is calculated as –25p/32.5p = –77% (32.5p being the average of the two prices)

Some of *The Times'* additional circulation reflects a minor expansion in the overall quality segment of the daily newspaper market during the period of price reductions. But most of its gains have come at the expense of rivals. Not all participants in the market have been affected. The circulations of two of the quality broadsheets – the *Guardian* and *Financial Times* – have been relatively unaffected by price warfare. 'Cross-elasticity of demand' measures the responsiveness of demand for one product to any change in the price of another. A low level of cross-elasticity of demand between either the *Guardian* or *Financial Times* and the remaining broadsheets suggests that, for these two titles, no close substitutes are perceived as being available.

However, other titles in the quality segment of the market have suffered considerably as a result of *The Times'* price-cutting strategy. Both the *Daily Telegraph* and, especially, the *Independent* have experienced reductions in circulation. Losses in circulation have been compounded by lower sales income caused by their own strategies of price discounting deployed in response to *The Times'* aggressive pricing policy. The evidence of cross-elasticity of demand between these three titles – *The Times, Daily Telegraph* and *Independent* – implies that levels of consumers' surplus for each is relatively low, at least amongst a proportion of their readers. The reductions in income suffered by the *Daily Telegraph* and *Independent* have been significant and, in the case of the *Independent*, have even threatened its continuation.

Rival firms have appealed to the UK competition authorities on several occasions on the grounds that News International is engaged in predatory pricing but these allegations have repeatedly been found to be 'not proven' (Reeves, 1998: 11). Predatory pricing occurs when a firm cuts the price of a product to below costs and keeps it there in order to drive rivals out of the market or to deter possible new entrants. *The Times* has been selling at a price below its costs and this appears to have forestalled the expansion of rivals and placed at least one in acute financial distress. On the other hand, *The Times* was a very unprofitable title before it embarked on price-cutting. The problem with proving allegations of predatory pricing against News International is that none of its rivals have actually been squeezed out of the market (at least, as yet) and, in any event, many national newspapers in the UK have a long history of making losses – i.e. of selling at below cost.

Any narrowing in the range of titles available to UK consumers as a result of News International's aggressive pricing strategies would clearly imply a welfare loss. But so long as aggressive pricing does not result in a restriction of choice and diversity then it does not appear to act against the public interest. Indeed, it may be argued that consumers have benefited from lower newspaper prices, at least in the short term. Yet even if aggressive pricing does not result in the actual elimination of rivals, the fact that it stunts their growth or forces them into financial difficulty may well threaten the quality of their output, with concomitant welfare implications.

SUCCESS OF TRANSNATIONAL MAGAZINE PUBLISHERS IN EUROPE

Magazine publishing is similar in many ways to newspaper publishing. As with newspapers, revenues are earned from advertising and from copy sales. Advertising is by far the more important of these two revenue sources for 'business' (or professional) magazines, as opposed to 'consumer' titles. Consumer magazines (those concerned with leisure, lifestyle, etc.), on the other hand, derive the majority of their income from cover sales (PPA, 2000: 4–5). Magazines are confronted by similar costs to newspapers – editorial, advertising sales, paper, printing, distribution, etc. – and, although print runs tend to be smaller, magazine publishing is strongly characterized by economies of scale.

One of the major differences between magazine and newspaper publishing is that the magazine industry is flourishing. Readership and revenues of magazines have generally been growing steadily throughout the last two decades. Average operating profit margins in the UK magazine publishing sector are much higher than in the newspaper industry (Schroder Business Ratios Report, 1999, cited in PPA, 2000: 10). Another important difference is that, whereas newspapers tend to concentrate on specific national or local markets and are usually very closely associated with these markets in terms of both copy sales and advertising, magazine publishing is much more international in its focus.

Very few European newspapers – the *Financial Times* provides a rare exception – are able to command any sizeable readership outside their own domestic markets. Likewise, only a tiny proportion of European-made television programmes are resold into European markets other than the ones for which they were originally made. As discussed in Chapters 5 and 6, international trade in audiovisual products is overwhelmingly dominated by US and not European suppliers. Magazines, however, are a success story for European producers. Magazines are virtually the only mass media product that European producers seem to be successful in selling beyond their own national boundaries. For example, the Burda publishing group, a German publishing company, publishes a fashion magazine called *Burda Moden* in 17 different countries and with an overall circulation of 4 million readers (Weymouth and Lamizet, 1996). *Elle* is published in 32 local editions and UK magazine publisher EMAP's *FHM* title is published in some 20 international territories.

'[M]agazine publishing has become increasingly international in character' in recent years (PPA, 2000: 88). Several studies have considered the factors which may help to explain this trend (Wedell and Luyken, 1986; Ostergaard, 1992; Hafstrand, 1995; Weymouth and Lamizet, 1996). First, magazines are not subject to the same cultural or political 'responsibilities' as other mass media products such as newspapers and especially broadcasting. Magazine publishers are free to publish whatever content they think will sell, and there is no public expectation that they should focus on national or local concerns. Content is not constrained by locality. Magazines are free to target and cater for the interests of transnational readership segments, and many do so very successfully, e.g. 'women's titles such as *Vogue, Cosmopolitan* and *Marie-Claire.*

Magazines are not subject to any technical constraints (e.g. 'frequency' or 'footprint' limits that affect the coverage of terrestrial and satellite broadcasters respectively) which might prevent transnational expansion. And, unlike broadcasting and newspapers, magazines are not subject to any special legislative barriers to growth which might prevent their penetration into other European or international markets. To preserve pluralism, many countries place restrictions on the extent to which owner-ship of radio and television broadcasting licences or newspapers may be held by foreign individuals or companies but magazines fall outside the general scope of these rules.

Language barriers can be relatively easy for magazine publishers to overcome because of the nature of the product and its content. This is particularly true of consumer as opposed to business titles. Consumer magazines tend to rely heavily on visual imagery such as photographs and are not tied down to specific national or regional audiences. Of course, many publications have a cultural specificity which makes it difficult just to cut and paste copy into versions suitable for alternative geographic markets (O' Connor, 2000a: 4). Nonetheless, adaptation of editorial content at a local level to meet the demands of particular market environ-ments is frequently a feasible option. For many magazines, local editions can be published or the title reprinted in other languages without necessarily losing any of the magazine's flavour or relevance.

A magazine's main asset is its title or brand. Consumer and business magazines work hard to create brand images 'which ensure that their readers continue to buy them every week or every month' (Gasson, 1996: 81). Often, the strength of the brand is sufficient to ensure that it will have some appeal for the same lifestyle group or niche in many different geographic (and different product) markets, even if some adaptation at the local level may be required. One of the growth strategies that is often deployed by successful magazine publishers is to launch new titles in overseas markets that capitalize on the brand strength of an established market leader in the home market.

So, the nature of the product and the absence of international barriers to trade provides magazine publishers with opportunities to sell their wares in other countries to particular lifestyle or professional groups. Some European publishers have been better placed than others to take advantage of these opportunities.

Levels of consumption of print media products vary by country and by linguistic region. Across Europe, circulation and readership levels tend to be strongest in Northern and especially German-language markets. At the other extreme, the Greek and Portuguese markets with their distinctive languages and poorer economies can only support a limited number of mass market titles. International data collected by the UK Advertising Association suggests that there is a positive correlation between countries where magazine circulations are highest per capita – i.e. Germany, the Netherlands and Switzerland – and countries with highest per capita expenditure on magazine advertising. The strength of German publishers in their own large domestic market has been instrumental in providing the resources needed for expansion into other territories. Germany not only has the highest domestic sales of magazines in Europe, but German publishers (especially Bauer, Burda and Gruner+Jahr) tend to own and publish more magazines in other countries than any other publishers.

Even so, transnational expansion is an increasingly common strategy in the sector and has been deployed successfully by, for example, many UK, French and US publishers. UK publisher EMAP has been expanding internationally since the early 1990s and is now a major player in France and the USA as well as in its own home market. According to Hafstrand (1995: 5), some of the main driving forces behind 'internationalization' are saturated home markets, 'the increased internationalization of the entire media business and shifting demands from the advertising market'.

Major publishers will seek out opportunities to expand internationally because, quite often, their own home markets are already mature and subject to intense competition. It may be less risky and more attractive to launch a tried-and-tested editorial format in a new territory than it is to seek out new formulas for the home market. International expansion may also be motivated by corporate circumstances. Magazine brands that fall into the ownership of transnational media corporations such as Time Warner or Condé Nast are very likely to be expanded and exploited internationally. In addition, Hafstrand points out that advertisers are increasingly keen on developing their own brands on a transnational if not 'global' level. This has encouraged magazine publishers to adopt expansion strategies appropriate to these needs.

SEGMENTATION OF DEMAND

An important feature of the way in which the magazine publishing industry has grown in recent years has been the trend towards increased segmentation of readership or increased subdivision of demand into more and more narrow specialisms. Segmentation is a marketing term that refers to the process of 'dividing the total market into groups or segments of customers with similar needs or preferences' (Shankar, 2001: 8). A number of issues explain why strategies of segmentation and targeting have become more prevalent in the magazine sector.

Looking first at changes affecting demand, two of the main factors which stimulate overall demand for consumer magazines are the amount of leisure time people have available to them and also their disposable incomes. Both of these variables were on the increase in many European countries in the late 1980s and, again, in the mid to late 1990s. The growth in disposable incomes, particularly in wealthier European countries, has brought with it increased demand, especially in middle and upper-market sectors, for higher quality entertainment, features and hobby magazines, such as photographic, sport, cooking and DIY publications.

To take advantage of these trends, many magazine publishers embarked on a strategy of launching new titles aimed at more specialized segments of the market. New titles appeared aimed at yachting enthusiasts, golf enthusiasts and so on rather than sports enthusiasts more generally. Titles aimed at 'women', 'men' or 'teenagers' became subdivided into numerous segments according to age, income, lifestyle and attitude. Changes that took place in the cost structure and economic organization of the printing industry during the 1980s reduced the costs of publishing high quality magazines. This made it possible to cater for increasingly fragmented consumer demand by launching new low circulation titles.

Up until the 1980s, major magazine publishers such as EMAP and IPC in the UK, Time Warner in the USA and Condé Nast or Hachette in France tended to produce and print a relatively higher proportion of large circulation titles. This strategy meant that magazine publishers relied quite heavily on economies of scale rather than economies of scope. But the arrival of desk-top publishing and other technological advances made it much cheaper to produce new titles with lower print runs. Magazine publishers could produce low circulation magazines on a cost-effective basis, so many new specialized consumer titles were introduced. Evidence of an acceleration in strategies of market segmentation can be found in the growing number of titles being published every year. In the UK, for example, the number of business titles grew by 23 per cent to 5,713 between 1989 and 1998 while, in the same period, the number of consumer titles grew by 27 per cent to 3,174 (British Rate & Data figures cited in PPA, 2000: 15)

Many of the new and more narrowly focused titles that have been launched are attractive vehicles for advertisers. Even so, an analysis of the breakdown in total expenditure on consumer magazines between cover sales and advertising over time shows a steady increase in the proportion of revenue derived from direct consumer purchases rather than from advertising (Figure 7.4). This change in the profile of publishers' income reflects the general shift towards greater circulation of more specialized monthlies, which tend to cost more (and whose prices have risen sharply since the late 1980s), and a corresponding decline in the share of general-interest weeklies, which tend to retail at a much lower cover price.

An important challenge for any newly launched magazine title is to survive long enough to justify the considerable investment and promotional costs involved in its launch (Gasson, 1996: 87). The vast majority of magazines have a limited life expectancy and success depends on whether the publisher has identified and valued the target market segment for that title correctly. To calculate the likely returns from the brand image created by the magazine title, publishers will not only take account of opportunities for domestic and international exploitation of the magazine but will also consider the potential to extend the brand across additional product markets. To ensure its survival, a magazine constantly needs to monitor and adapt its editorial and brand image to ensure it maintains an economically viable constituency.

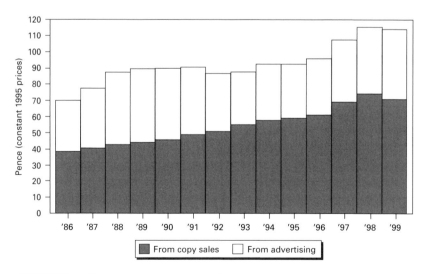

FIGURE 7.4   Consumer magazines: publishers' net revenue per copy sold, 1986–99 (Advertising Association, 2000: 134)

Strategies of targeting or segmentation are clearly at the heart of the consumer and business magazine publishing sectors. Segmentation of audiences or readership into sub-national specialist groups allows the industry to expand its products overseas in a way that other mass media often find difficult. Segmentation can be seen as a unique strength of the magazine publishing sector in terms of offering convenient and cost-effective access to particular audiences. The ability to target narrow specialist interest, lifestyle and professional groups is an obvious selling point with advertisers.

An advantageous feature of segmentation is that it creates possible synergies with other commercial activities. For example, 'masthead' television programmes (i.e. programmes based on particular magazines) can not only capitalize on a magazine's established brand appeal but may also provide 'enticing possibilities for sharing editorial and production costs' (Wood, 1998: 14). Many successful magazine publishers have used their expertise in communicating with specific segments of the population to develop complementary products and services. Several are involved in organizing exhibitions, trade fairs and databases that target the same specialist audience groups as their magazine titles.

EMAP's strategy is to try to get 'a multimedia platform for very strong brands', according to Chris Llewellyn.[3] The brands in question are, of course, titles such as *FHM*, *Q* and *Smash Hits* which, in the guise of magazines, have achieved enormous success with their target markets. The aim is to transpose the success of such brands onto additional complementary goods and services that extend the publisher's relationship with the consumer and the advertiser. EMAP has diversified from magazine publishing into radio broadcasting and electronic publishing and is beginning to develop television activities. The company is also active in business communications, organization of shows and trade fairs and provision of database services. Diversification has allowed EMAP to approach exploitation of its brands and its associations with specific audience segments in a more flexible or 'media neutral' way.

Conversely, the 'media neutral' approach implies that magazines are increasingly vulnerable to threats from alternative media. Thematic channels and specialist subscription-based services exemplify the encroachment of television into 'narrowcasting'. The growth of electronic dissemination, peer-to-peer networking and other Internet services aimed

---

3. Citations from a guest lecture to the MSc in Media Management class at the University of Stirling on 10 November 2000 by Chris Llewellyn, International Publishing Director of EMAP plc.

at special interest groups has introduced another set of competitors. Magazines are no longer the only bridge between narrow audience segments and advertisers. New interactive media services are bringing competition both for consumers' attention and for specialist advertising.

eight

NEW MEDIA

N ew production and distribution technologies have a significant and ongoing impact on the economics of the media. This chapter explores the transformative influence of digitization and the development of electronic infrastructures for delivery of media. The economic implications of increased overlap between media, telecommunications and computing and the growth of Internet-based media provision are examined.

After studying this chapter, you should be able to:

- Understand how digitization is affecting media content creation
- Analyse the economics of online media provision
- Understand the importance of copyright protection for electronic distribution

WHAT'S NEW ABOUT 'NEW' MEDIA?

Like other sectors of economic activity that are heavily reliant on technology, the media industry seems permanently subject to advancement and change. In recent decades, new cable and satellite technology has facilitated a vast expansion in broadcast distribution. The explosive growth of new broadcast channels has generally not been matched by increased viewing and listening but, instead, has brought a progressive fragmentation of mass audiences. Likewise, new encryption technology has contributed to segmentation and fragmentation of audiences as direct viewer payments have become available to fund niche or thematic television services.

Today, the development of digital technology is the great 'new' force affecting the media and it has implications for virtually all aspects of the industry. Digitization denotes the move towards storing, reproducing and transmitting pieces of media content in the form of digits in a binary code consisting of zeros and ones. One major implication of this new technology is that media content of any kind, once reduced to digits, can more readily be manipulated and repackaged for dissemination in another guise or format. Hence, digitization has contributed to some blurring of conventional product market boundaries in the media. Another important issue is that digital compression techniques allow for a much more efficient use of bandwidth; a far greater volume and range of services can be conveyed digitally than was possible using analogue technology.

So the spread of digital technology is affecting media production, distribution and consumption patterns, with knock-on effects for advertising. Digitization has also facilitated a greater 'convergence' or overlap in the technologies used by the broadcasting, telecommunications and computing sectors. An increasing number of homes are connected to high capacity communication networks and are using the Internet through their PCs, telephones and, in some cases, their television sets.

THE INTERNET AND E-COMMERCE

The Internet is, of course, based on digital technology and provides a marketplace for electronic commerce or e-commerce. Broadly speaking, electronic commerce involves 'the use of electronic means and technologies to conduct commerce, including within-business, business-to-business and business-to-consumer interactions' (Choi et al., 1997: 13). The Internet is also widely used for non-commercial activities such as research and exchanging personal e-mail. But e-commerce is about businesses using electronic technology to try to make money, although many Internet start-ups have spectacularly failed to do so.

The Net is often promoted as a means for businesses to lower their costs and improve their efficiency in various ways. It speeds up communication and information flows and can be used by firms to provide staff, suppliers and prospective customers with access to information about products, processes and services. The Internet also provides a potentially lucrative forum for buying and selling: for example the online retailing of books, CDs and travel services. According to a recent survey in the *Economist*, e-commerce accounted for 1 per cent of total sales in the USA in the year

2000 but 'is growing rapidly' as Amazon and eBay, among others, become household names (2000: 10).

Thanks to digitization, media content is ideally suited to dissemination over the Internet. The Net represents an additional or alternative distribution platform for all sorts of media content and services. Whereas electronic retailers of regular material goods such as books and CDs generally face significant marginal supply and delivery costs, the nature of most news and entertainment content is such that it can be digitized and conveyed directly over the Internet in a format suitable for users and at relatively little marginal cost.

The opportunities associated with the growth of the Net have had a marked effect on the development of media players and their products over the last few years. Most media firms with a strategy for exploiting the Internet have taken the view that it involves not just offering the same old media goods and content electronically, but also the creation of 'new' and differentiated products which reflect and suit modes of consumer interface on the Net. A range of additional products has begun to emerge, many of which combine different media (e.g. audiovisual images plus text) and embrace the increasingly important concept of interactivity. Indeed, many of the high profile corporate deals that have taken place in the sector in recent times (including, most notably, the AOL/Time Warner merger in 2000) have involved marriages of 'old' and 'new' media players specifically intended to capitalize on this new infrastructure.

Home broadband connections continue to increase in 2001, though there are indications that the rate at which new businesses and users are joining the Internet has started to slow down in the USA and the UK. Added to this, the recent cooling off of investor interest in dot.com businesses has been accompanied by a mood of scepticism concerning the capabilities of the Internet and the prospects for e-commerce. However, so long as the broadband technology supporting the Internet is improving and its audience is growing, the opportunities associated with conveying media content through this infrastructure continue to hold great promise.

DIGITIZED MEDIA CONTENT

Perhaps the most significant effect of digitization is a progressive expansion in distribution outlets for media. Digital compression techniques have multiplied the potential number of broadcast channels and the Internet provides a virtually unlimited forum for publishing, broadcast and narrowcast transmissions, multimedia and interactive services of all kinds. So, increasing demand for content and the changing interests of the current generation of children who are growing up with the Internet, WAP and digital television – so-called 'Generation @' – are providing unprecedented creative and commercial opportunities for media content producers.

Digital technology is bringing down production costs. In the audiovisual sector, the arrival of low-cost digital cameras, camcorders and editing equipment capable of producing broadcast-quality output has made production cheaper and lowered barriers to industry entry. The replacement of analogue with digital technology is not only lowering capital equipment costs but is also reducing the number of technicians required to make audiovisual content. For television broadcasters, the lowering of production costs has made it more economically feasible to produce content aimed at narrow audience segments.

In terms of film, digital technology has dramatically reduced the potential cost of making feature-length productions. The critical success achieved by Danish film-makers Dogme in the late 1990s for such low-budget features as *Festen* has drawn considerable attention to the possibilities opened up by digital technology. In 1999, the much-publicized commercial success at the box-office of *The Blair Witch Project* – made on a shoestring budget using hand-held camcorders – underlined the way in which digitization has lowered costs and reduced technology-based entry barriers into the film production industry.

INCREASED ECONOMIES OF SCALE AND SCOPE

Digitization makes it possible to reduce images, sounds and text to a common format and to transport these via a common distribution infrastructure. This has facilitated a convergence of previously discrete sectors of the media. The fact that content, when reduced to digital 'metadata', can be stored, manipulated, reformatted and repackaged with much greater ease than before has significant implications for its exploitation and for the economics of content production and distribution.

Economies of scale are clearly an important feature in the production of media content, including by digital means. 'Digital product requires a large initial investment to produce the first unit . . . [but] the per-unit cost decreases as the number of units sold increases' (Choi et al., 1997: 466). Any expansion in consumption of a given digital media product or service will generally result in an increase in profitability per unit of output; economies of scale will accrue because of low marginal costs.

So, maximizing the available market for the firm's output is an obvious goal for the digital content creator. But since tastes and preferences are not entirely homogeneous across the full potential market, some additional (specialized) inputs may well be required to induce additional experimentation with and consumption of the firm's output. In other words, marginally 'differentiated' products make sense, at least to the point where marginal revenues exceed costs. With digital technology, the cost of producing marginally differentiated media products can be much reduced. Digitization has therefore increased the economies available to content-creators as they seek to expand their markets.

The spread of digital technology means that successful media brands can be exploited across different distribution platforms and in different formats much more easily. Increasingly, content-producers can be viewed as multi-product firms. This is encouraging not only changes in strategy but also, in some cases, changes of name. For example, UK television production company Invincible Films became 'multi-platform content creator' Narrateo just ahead of an equity offering in autumn 2000 (Derecki, 2000). For the multi-product firm, a distinction can be made between economies of scale – i.e. cost-efficiencies created as the scale of consumption of a given range of products expands – and economies of scope- i.e. cost-efficiencies which arise as the mix of output changes. The benefits of digital technology are greatly magnified because of the co-existence, for media content, of both economies of scale and of scope.

It is sometimes argued that the spread of digital will serve to equalize opportunity for small companies as well as established media giants. Digitization and the growth of the Internet are indeed reducing many barriers to market entry and creating opportunities for smaller enterprises and firms offering skills in new forms of content creation (such as computer games). However, the digital environment favours strong and recognizable brands. In the words of one UK publishing executive, 'brands make it easier for the customer to make choices as the world gets more complicated'.[1] Without recognizable brands and worthwhile levels of consumer awareness, potential newcomers to the online universe may well find that the high initial costs involved in establishing an online presence (typically involving extensive campaigns on conventional media) represent an effective deterrent to market entry. Large and established media content providers with strong brands and access to valuable back catalogues of images, text and sound have several advantages when it comes to exploitation of the additional scale economies made possible by digitization.

The exploitation of content in a digital environment raises questions about how best to manage content. Media suppliers need efficient systems and processes to manage their digital assets. In order to make the most

---

1. Citation from Chris Llewellyn, International Publishing Director of EMAP plc, 10 November 2000.

of the new technology, companies need to be able 'to capture, store, manage, exploit and protect assets digitally, at the level of granularity of the smallest consumable unit' (Bowler, 2000: 7). By capturing text, images, etc. digitally during the initial creation process, the later stages of archiving, editing, manipulation and packaging of content can be carried out more easily and cost-effectively.

Firms that, for example, want to repackage back libraries or transform elements of their current catalogue into new products and services have need of a speedy and convenient means of accessing and reformatting their content. Until very recently, this would have been a labour-intensive process involving several stages, physical movement of product and the production of support material. But a variety of software packages are now evolving which facilitate the storage, transfer and transformation of products and brands in a digital context. Automated content management systems will enable content-creators and rights owners to protect their assets from physical degradation and will improve their ability to extract maximum commercial value from the content they own.

INTERACTIVITY

Digitization is not only about re-use of media content but is also about the creation of new sorts of content for 'new' media products. Digital technology allows for greater amounts of data or more layers of content to be packed into a product, paving the way for a more sophisticated array of multimedia and interactive goods and services. In professional information publishing, for example, the capability of the Internet to allow searches for specific or related pieces of information has led to the development of new services which are interactive and more closely focused on meeting the needs of individual customers. Digital broadcasting has also resulted in more interactive and customer-centred services, for example video-on-demand (VOD) and near-video-on-demand, i.e. offering viewers the opportunity to pay to watch a range of movies a short time after their box-office release.

Despite much hype about interactive television (iTV), the medium is still in its infancy, with only a small handful of services set up in countries including France, Spain and the UK. Early debate tended to focus on which sort of delivery platform – whether satellite, digital terrestrial or cable – would be best suited to conveying iTV. In theory, cable television has an advantage because the capability for two-way communication between the broadcaster and viewer is inbuilt and permanent. However, interactivity is generally not a problem now for other types of broadcasters because the 'return path' from the viewer to the broadcaster (which makes the service interactive) can be provided by means of a conventional modem attached to the television set and a telephone line. Indeed, the potential to offer iTV is attracting interest not only from conventional broadcasters but also from other infrastructure providers (e.g. telecommunications operators and ISPs), content-producers and even electronic retailers.

The major question now is: do consumers really want iTV and what sort of services will prove to be economically viable? The results of early trials for VOD and NVOD in the USA and Europe have proved encouraging in terms of viewer demand. The other main possibilities include so-called 't-commerce' – home shopping via the television set; interactive game shows – allowing television viewers to participate in game shows; 'enhanced TV' – providing extra information, different camera angles, etc.; and VOD.

In the UK, BSkyB's Open service – since named BSkyB Interactive – was launched in 2000, offering a range of interactive services including online shopping and banking, e-mail and games. Shopping via the television set is still a very novel concept in the UK and has certainly not yet achieved the levels of acceptance exhibited, for example, in the USA. However, a 'significant uplift' in sales of toys and seasonal gifts via iTV was noted in the UK in the run-up to Christmas 2000 (Ody, 2000: 17). Woolworth's, for example, recorded around 5,000 orders per week on Open during this period and expects plenty of growth in orders in 2001 (Rothwell, 2000: 28). Digital television can also offer a 'walled garden' of interactive services similar to those available on the Net (e.g. online banking). Indeed, some commentators expect t-commerce to expand rapidly and to overtake e-commerce through the PC within the next few years (Foremski, 2000:11).

Some UK television subscribers have experienced 'interactivity' while using their TV sets to send and receive e-mail. A minority are also using their TVs to access the Net, though the PC provides the predominant mode of Internet access in the UK as elsewhere. Using the TV screen to access the Internet is not ideal. 'Most internet pages are designed to be viewed on a PC screen rather than on a TV and while pages for TV can be designed using the same HTML language as the web, it is difficult to turn a web page into one that looks good on television' (Larsen, 2000). In spite of these drawbacks, it is argued that because many people are reluctant to purchase PCs for home access to the Internet, the TV will eventually prove the more popular means for going online (Rothwell, 2000: 27).

The popularity of the first Channel Four fly-on-the-wall documentary/ game-show series *Big Brother* in the UK in summer 2000 clearly demonstrated the potential for digitization and iTV to add to the viewing experience. *Big Brother* was simulcast live on the Net, allowing viewers to tune in at any time and follow events in the shared house before and after nightly terrestrial broadcasts. As the series progressed, many viewers flocked to the *Big Brother* website which was 'propelled into the UK's top 30 with a unique audience of 874,000 in July' (Sheldon, 2000: 7). Viewers were given the opportunity to interact with the website through chatlines and given options to view events in the house via different hidden cameras. Millions of viewers also participated in the programme by casting votes by telephone each week about which of the house-mates ought to be evicted.

The phenomenal success of the *Big Brother* format appears to have owed much to its interactive dimension, which generated high levels of involvement on the part of viewers. It is not yet clear which other programme genres will benefit from incorporating interactivity but much experimentation remains centred around game shows. In the USA, television viewers can play along with *Who Wants To Be A Millionaire* from the abc.com website and, in the UK, Channel Four launched a second series of *Big Brother* in May 2001. Both BSkyB and ITV Digital have extended the concept by teaming up with gambling group Blue Square to develop services that offer UK viewers the opportunity to bet on sporting events while watching them on television.

By and large, however, experiments with interactivity have tended to be confined to the provision of some extra information or other 'enhanced' options alongside a conventional television broadcast which viewers may call up while watching a programme. For example, some sports channels have tried offering extra camera angles, replays and statistics via digital television. Broadcasters have yet to identify how to make the most of interactivity. But consumer surveys have been of little assistance because most people still have trouble conceiving of their television as an interactive device. One UK cable industry executive compared asking viewers what iTV services they would like to 'asking them what controls they want on their spaceship' (cited in Larsen, 2000: 2).

A problem facing interactive audiovisual content producers is that, generally speaking, consumers tend to have different expectations when they sit down to watch television than when they hook up to the Internet. For many, television is still about relaxation and passive entertainment, and operating the remote control device is about as much interactivity as is desired. 'Surfing the Net' is a pro-active experience requiring constant interaction and engagement on the part of the user. But television is expected to be fast, slick and entertaining. Even amongst television producers, opinions are divided about the prospects for interactive drama. Some believe that 'dramatic narrative should be left to the experts [while] . . . the rest of us are just there to be passively entertained', while others 'passionately believe that audience participation is the future' (O'Rorke, 2001: 58).

At the moment, the ability for two-way communication between the viewer and the broadcaster still seems to be under-exploited. The current generation of children who are growing up with the Internet, WAP and digital television will undoubtedly play an important part in defining how the attributes of interactivity can best be exploited by commercial broadcasters. Meanwhile, several tools are being created which will help viewers to manage 'smart TV' and embrace interactivity, such as interactive programme guides (IPGs) and personal video recorders (PVRs).

A study by Forrester Research indicated that IPGs were in use in 34 million US households in the year 2000 and around 750,000 had acquired PVRs by the end of the year (Bernhoff, 2000: 10). A further 5 million viewers in the USA use interactive video devices – i.e. set-top boxes with a built-in modem which allow viewers to interact with transmissions of programmes and advertisements (e.g. Wink or Microsoft's WebTV Plus boxes). In general, these tools enable viewers to select and create their own schedules of programmes and they are playing a useful role in educating viewers about the benefits of interactivity. As these devices gain wider acceptance, the next stage, according to Forrester, is that broadcasters will develop and offer more 'smart' output – i.e. transmissions which include in their metadata information about content and duration as well as potential interactive links (Bernhoff, 2000: 11).

PERSONALIZATION

Along with interactivity, 'personalization' has become a key word – viewers taking control, exercising personal choice and self-scheduling. Arguably, this should result in an improved experience for media consumers. Customized consumption is clearly better suited to certain forms of media than others. The opportunity for individually tailored media works best where the user has very specific tastes and interests or informational needs to satisfy.

Professional information publishing – provision of news, information and analysis about specific industry sectors – provides an example of a media product whose customer base is generally very interested in tailoring its consumption. Until recently, professional information publishers have tended to disseminate their content only in the form of reports, newsletters and periodicals. But digitization has paved the way for publishers to provide more personalized information services to their customers and this has resulted in a marked restructuring of their businesses with a greater focus on the customer. 'The arrival of the Internet has enabled [professional information publishers] . . . to increase the service element of their content massively, through bundling together rafts of related products, interlinking them and making them cross-researchable' (Gasson, 2001: 50).

The opportunities for more personalized media consumption are forcing media companies across the board to consider how to adapt their businesses. The provision of additional thematic, niche or specialist services on a paid-for basis is an obvious response, provided that market demand will support this strategy. But not all media are financed by direct payments from the consumer and, as discussed in Chapter 3, the fragmentation of mass audiences caused by more personalized media consumption has worrying implications for advertiser-supported media.

HOW DOES THE INTERNET AFFECT THE ECONOMICS OF MEDIA COMPANIES?

The volume of data embedded in many new media products and services – e.g. iTV, multimedia and interactive computer games – is such that, even using compression technologies, they require extensive bandwidth in order to be conveyed at reasonable speed and quality. So, for the full range of possibilities opened up by digitization and the Net to be realized, a majority of the population of Internet users needs to be linked up via high-capacity broadband cable connections.

The infrastructure on which the Internet is conveyed is constantly being upgraded but it has still not arrived at the point where 'webcasting' (transmitting video programmes over the Net) is widespread. Video images which have been compressed for transmission along the Net generally tend to look small and jerky on a PC screen. In the UK, the relatively slow spread of upgraded broadband cable connections in the all-important 'last mile' to the home has been attributed to reticence on the part of BT to allow rivals into the market (Teather, 2001: 52) . Elsewhere across Europe and in the USA, connections between the Internet and the home are generally improving with more installations of high data-speed DSL (digital subscriber line) telephony facilities. And, as more and more homes are wired with the broadband cable needed for affordable high-bandwidth services, the Internet is destined to become a much more formidable force in terms of audiovisual, multimedia and interactive media services.

The effect of the Net on media companies is, to some extent, the same as for firms in other industrial sectors. Like many technological innovations, its main virtue is that it lowers costs. The Internet speeds up and improves communication and information flows, both within a company and between the company and its suppliers and customers. So the Internet yields several gains, including lower communication costs, time savings and reduced business-to-business transaction costs (i.e. the Net has generally made it easier to find the cheapest supplier of any product or service the firm may need).

For media companies, especially those involved in news and factual content provision, improved access to information sources represents a useful benefit. Widespread publication on the Net of data of all kinds on virtually every topic has greatly reduced the cost of what is an essential function for many media companies – information gathering.

The Internet has also come to represent a potentially very important promotional tool for companies, and the websites of media companies feature strongly amongst those most frequently visited. Media firms generally have a competitive advantage when it comes to website design since media content captured digitally (video, text, audio, graphics, logos, etc.) can easily be translated into promotional website features.

But the crucial way in which the Internet affects media companies is that it is, in itself, a distribution platform. The fact that media content can be reduced to a string of zeros and ones and distributed electronically means that it is ideally suited to dissemination over the Net. Of course, this is also true of other knowledge-based intangible goods, for example computer software. The general implication is that the growth of the Internet represents an opportunity to distribute media content either as existing or as new products over an additional delivery platform at a very low marginal cost.

Many major media companies have invested heavily in positioning themselves as providers of content on the Internet and some (such as the BBC) have already established strong online brands. Publishers including Reed Elsevier, EMAP, Trinity Mirror and Pearson have announced plans to spend hundreds of millions of pounds over the next three years in a variety of Net-based projects and commercial television broadcasters have also been spending considerable sums on the introduction of additional web-based services.

Inasmuch as the Internet offers opportunities, it also threatens the livelihood of some conventional media. Publishers of text-based specialist information are particularly prone to competition from free websites, peer-to-peer e-mail networks, etc. The Internet has proved especially well suited as a medium for classified advertising (e.g. recruitment) . So it already poses a considerable threat to media players who have traditionally dominated the targeted classified advertising sector – namely, newspaper and magazine publishers. In the UK, for example, regional newspapers derive more than half of their revenue from classified advertising. And, as the capacity for webcasting becomes a more commonplace reality, the ongoing fragmentation of television audiences will also pose significant challenges for broadcasters.

DERIVING REVENUES FROM THE NET

> I just don't see how you can make money out of it. (Rupert Murdoch, cited in Martinson, 2001b)

In theory, the opportunity to distribute media products at a very low marginal cost over an additional and increasingly popular high-capacity delivery platform should herald a bonanza for media companies. In practice, the vast majority of media operators have found it practically impossible to make any money from investments in the Internet, inter-activity and new multimedia products. This has resulted in an abrupt and fairly widespread withdrawal or reduction of resources from Internet-based media ventures since autumn 2000 by companies such as EMAP and News International.

To some extent at least, current difficulties with securing returns on new media investments reflect the climate of euphoric expectation in which many decisions were taken by media companies to develop their online activities and to buy strategic stakes in Internet start-ups. For example, shares in BSkyB rose by 30 per cent in February 2000 after it announced an investment in developing its online activities. Likewise, shares in Reuters jumped by 30 per cent (adding £6 billion to the company's market capitalisation) when it announced plans to invest £0.5 billion on transferring its business information activities online over the next few years (O'Connor, 2000b: 26). Few publicly quoted media companies escaped shareholder pressure to put into place ambitious Internet invest-ment programmes that, with hindsight, have begun to look somewhat hasty.

The underlying problem with Internet-based media provision as an economic activity is that few if any realistic models have been constructed for deriving revenues from it which are adequate to cover the costs of the service in question. On the issue of the costs which must be covered, the evidence so far is that marginal operating expenses associated with offering web-based versions of established products (e.g. online magazines or newspapers) are often anything but negligible. For example, until recently some 400 additional staff were employed at the *New York Times* to produce its online version (Martinson, 2001a). On top of this, a heavy initial investment in building up the brand and following for the online product has to be repaid over time.

Theoretically, economies of scale and scope provide a compelling case in favour of offering media content online. But to reap such economies, the marginal costs associated with supplying the product over the Internet must be held in check. Judging by the relatively lavish (by comparison with prospective revenues) scale of human and other resources dedicated by media companies to developing parallel and new online activities, this logic seems to have been fairly widely ignored, at least until the dot.com collapse of autumn 2000. But now that the race to establish an online presence at any cost has subsided, questions about the viability of Internet-based media businesses have come to the fore.

At least three possible streams of income are potentially available to the online media provider. The first of these is advertising. Internet sites conveying, for example, online magazines can offer both classified and display advertising. 'Banners' or graphics that pop up at the top or bottom of the screen of most content sites account for the majority of Internet advertisements and these are deemed to have done their job if a visitor clicks on the banner and is taken to the appropriate page. Internet advertising is growing much faster than advertising on other media and, in the USA, 'is already bigger than outdoor' (Zenith Media, 2001: 2). Not surprisingly, the main spenders tend to be technology companies and other Internet businesses.

But, by and large, advertising is simply not generating enough money to cover the costs of offering free services online. So, some online media providers seek to supplement advertising by tapping into a second valuable source of revenue – namely, e-commerce. The media-content supplier can arrange direct links to sell the items it is advertising, or goods that are reviewed or referred to on the site. For example, a feature on current fashion or music in EMAP's web-based magazine *FHM.co.uk* might give browsers the opportunity to 'click-though' to purchase the items mentioned in the article. Purchases made in this way can earn the online media provider more in sales commissions than it receives through advertising.

The third available option is to charge users a fee in return for access to online media. The direct charge is an attractive option for the media supplier insofar as it reduces exposure to the cyclicality of advertising income. From the user's point of view, however, direct charges are not so attractive. With some '1.5m pages published for free on the Internet every day' (Gasson, 2001: 50), most users exhibit considerable reluctance to pay for access to information or entertainment over the Net. Some narrowly focused (e.g. special interest publishing) services do, in fact, manage to attract subscriptions. The *Wall Street Journal's* online version – *wsj.com* – had 535,000 subscribers as at December 2000, each paying an annual subscription of $29. Even so, *wsj.com* is losing money and is not expected to break even until 2002 at the earliest (Martinson, 2001b).

For the majority of existing online media products and services, direct charges seem to be either unworkable or not the best option. The online business news and information service offered by Pearson's *FT.com*, for example, requires users to register but is then provided free. Most registered users are not regular *Financial Times* readers so the introduction of direct charges could potentially yield some additional sales revenue for the group. On the other hand, offering the service free over the Net ensures that the audience for *Financial Times* content is maximized and, since its demographic profile both online and offline is '25–54s, mostly male and seriously upmarket', *FT.com* is likely to earn substantial income from advertising (Zenith Media, 2001: 118).

For those online products and services which do rely on a direct charge, it is clearly essential that access to whatever valuable content subscribers are paying for is not made available free of charge elsewhere. The potential for widespread intermediation of data across the Internet (i.e. for reassembling or repackaging of content posted at other websites) poses a considerable threat to the livelihood of online publishers. Electronic piracy, or illegal reproduction of copyright protected works, is also a major concern.

ELECTRONIC DISTRIBUTION AND COPYRIGHT

The issue of copyright protection exemplifies how conventional economic theories often do not work well for media. Economics is the science of 'not being able to have it both ways' and is firmly predicated on the notion of scarcity. The production of two of anything is supposed to be more expensive than the production of one. However, electronic reproduction of media content costs little or nothing. A new music album may cost millions of pounds to create, but making extra copies of it costs next to nothing, especially if these are distributed over the Internet.

The laws of economics would have it that an 'optimal' or ideal situation has been achieved only when it is not possible, through any reorganization of available resources, to make anyone better off without making someone else worse off. This implies that inefficiencies are created every time someone is denied access to copyright-protected intellectual property. Providing free access to a copyright-protected product for those who would otherwise be unwilling or unable to pay for it would add positively to the sum of human welfare and would do so, it may be argued, without making anyone worse off. So, to avoid a sub-optimal allocation of resources, copyright protection ought not to be enforced.

This is all well and good as far as those who wish to consume copyright-protected works for free are concerned. However, the purpose of copyright is to establish a commercial incentive for authors, musicians, media producers, etc. to produce creative output. The creators of media content need to earn a living from their work and the guaranteed right to monopolise the earnings generated by their output for a certain time period is vital to the process. Without proper enforcement of copyright, the quality and quantity of creative output would naturally deteriorate and societal welfare would suffer accordingly. So, notwithstanding 'unnecessary' welfare losses, there are very powerful counter-arguments to support maintenance of copyright protection.

The arguments, in principle, in favour of and against copyright protection are in no way affected by the spread of digitization or the arrival of new media. Easier reproduction and extra distribution platforms have no bearing on whether or not writers, musicians or film-makers ought to be allowed to monopolise the returns from their work. But policing copyright protection has become more difficult with the spread of new media technologies. The challenges associated with preserving copyright in the context of digitization and the Internet are increasing all the time. Enforcement problems – as exemplified by the case of Napster and the music industry – have serious implications for the economics of media content production and publishing.

LESSONS FROM NAPSTER

The Napster case centres on a computer program for swapping files developed by US student Shawn Fanning in 1999. Initially developed as a means of exchanging and sharing music recordings between friends, the Napster software program has since been used by millions of Internet surfers to download songs and the Napster website is credited with winning over 'more new customers in less time than any other service in history' (Harding, 2001a: 32). The term 'customer' might be questioned, however, since the great attraction of Napster has been that it enables users to download music off the Net for free.

Napster works on the basis of what is called peer-to-peer (P2P) networking. P2P enables public or private user groups who share a similar interest – or peers – to swap files with each other. Members connect into the network, publish a list of contents that they are willing to share on the Napster server and then a search function enables them to find out who else is online and what is available for downloading at any given moment in time. So, Napster serves as an enormous search and exchange facility where individuals post their own offerings for all other users to pick from. The essence of the service is that it allows consumers to access the hard drives of other Napster users and to download songs (stored on MP3 computer files) onto their own PCs or digital music appliances at no charge. Effectively, it provides convenient and speedy access for

Internet users to a vast array of copyright-protected music which, at least until the Summer of 2001, they could help themselves to for free.

The ability to charge consumers in return for recorded products which give access to songs (i.e. CDs, etc.) is crucial to the economics of the music industry. Napster is not the first technological innovation to pose a threat to record companies' ability to extract that charge. Earlier technological innovations, such as the tape-recorder, have undoubtedly encouraged some illegal copying and a concomitant diversion of revenues from the music industry. But the opportunity to make perfect digital copies combined with the speed and ease of downloading over the Internet has created the potential for violation of copyright on a wholly unprecedented scale.

Record companies have been amongst the first to bear the brunt of peer-to-peer networking but they are by no means alone in their vulnerability. The same sort of risk exists for any sector or firm whose product can be reduced to bits and bytes. This includes all forms of media output including text-based, audio, audiovisual and multimedia. Any information that can be reduced to a digital format and put into a computer file can be swapped and shared. The implications of P2P in the music industry for content creators in other sectors were summed up by Ken Berry, Chief Executive of EMI (one of the five major record companies), in the following terms: 'If . . . people think it is OK to steal music, then it will affect every area of the entertainment industry. Everything is going on the Internet: movies, TV, computer software, computer games, you name it' (cited in Harding, 2000: 27).

In order to fight back against the rapid growth of music file-swapping and illegal copying, the major record companies have joined forces with independent labels to bring a series of high-profile legal actions based on copyright infringement against Napster and other music service operators on the Net. Generally, the US courts have tended to support the record companies by clamping down on free downloads of music from sites that use the MP3 digital standard.

For example, a suit brought against the MyMP3 service, the website which takes its name from the MP3 software format, by the Recording Industry Association of America (RIAA) resulted in a New York court ruling in April 2000 that MP3.com was indeed liable for copyright infringement. Funded primarily by advertising, MP3 offers a 'music locker' service that enables users to access digital files of their favourite songs on any computer connected to the Net. The court did not accept MP3.com's argument that, because it only allows consumers to make copies of CDs they already own, their website does not actually infringe copyright. Consequently, to keep the MyMP3 service in business, MP3.com had to agree to pay major record companies Sony, Warner Music,

EMI and BMG some damages and a fee in return for ongoing use of their music (Heavens, 2000: 25).[2]

Most attention, however, has focused on Napster. The Napster service has developed a much larger customer base than any other Internet service of any kind – it had some 38 million members as at February 2001 (Laube, 2001: 12) – and it continues to grow with incredible speed. The back catalogues of the majority of well-established record companies have been made available for free not only via the Napster website but also at the websites of dozens of imitators, so 'the drain [of revenues] has already started' (Solomons, 2000: 2). This affects the value of music assets. Across the music industry, there is acute awareness of the implications in terms of future revenues that may be lost to illegal copying and file-sharing.

The defence put forward by Napster is that it cannot be held liable for the copyright violations carried out by people who use its system. Record companies, however, take the view that Napster is clearly encouraging widespread theft of intellectual property which belongs to themselves and their artists. Some prominent artists – most notably Lars Ulrich, of heavy metal band Metallica – have joined forces with the record companies in suing Napster for copyright violation. In a television interview, Ulrich voiced the following opinion about online file-sharing: 'If you can download my music for free then, let's say if you're a plumber or a car mechanic or whatever, I have the right to call you up anytime and demand that you fix my plumbing for free'.[3]

Ulrich makes the point that, just as in any other occupation or industry, musicians and record companies depend on being paid for their work. Copyright provides a mechanism for artists to secure payment from those who enjoy their output and, for Ulrich, enforcing payment for access to music is no different from enforcing payment for any other service. The analogy is flawed however, because it makes no distinction between the public- and the private-good attributes of cultural output versus plumbing services. Whereas plumbers and car mechanics will generally encounter very high direct marginal costs associated with providing their services, there are few if any costs associated with reproducing copyright-protected material electronically.

In addition, many would argue that file-swappers use sites like Napster merely as a source to sample music rather than to avoid purchasing it (Rigby, 2000: 17). If this is so then the proliferation of online file-sharing is, in fact, helping to promote music and it serves to encourage

2. Seagram's Universal Music Group still has an outstanding claim for damages against MP3.com.
3. Quotation from a short BBC documentary entitled *That Thing*, broadcast on BBC2 on 16 September 2000.

more rather than fewer legitimate purchases of music products. At this early stage, the precise impact of Internet music sites on overall demand for legitimate recordings has not yet been evaluated.[4] However, most record companies have adopted a pessimistic view and argue that, by reducing the music industry's earnings, electronic copyright violation threatens to deplete the resources available to nurture, replenish and sustain musical output.

Music publishing, like film-making, is an expensive and, to a certain extent, risky business. Record companies tend to take on a fairly wide variety of artists in the hope of capturing the next commercial success story. The hits that generate enormous income constitute only a small proportion of most record companies' repertoires but these are essential to cover the costs involved in backing an array of average and weak revenue performers. So the current system of remuneration, whereby fans go out to record shops and spend heavily on popular CDs, cassettes, etc., facilitates some risk-spreading within the industry.

The handful of hits that generate recurrent revenues are relied upon by record companies to help offset inevitable losses elsewhere and to provide the resources needed to develop new artists. But Napster's file-sharing technology threatens to make it much more difficult for the industry to derive recurrent revenues from hits and from back catalogues (Solomons, 2000: 2). Consequently, the record industry has waged a vigorous campaign to close Napster down on the basis that the service encourages widespread copyright infringement, to the detriment of artists and fans as well as the record companies themselves.

Many music fans have come to regard the legal tussle between Napster and the major record companies as 'cyberspace's version of David and Goliath' (Rigby, 2000: 17). Some have expressed hope that free distribution of music over the Internet might loosen the record industry's grip on artists and profits and that it could help to 'democratize' the industry. Aspiring artists might, for example, gain recognition for their work by posting it on Internet music sites.

But the evidence so far is that very few aspiring stars have been helped along by free distribution of music over the Internet. Notwithstanding the burgeoning growth of P2P networking and music file-sharing, it is still record companies who are active in finding, developing and promoting new artists. And, under the industry's existing business model, their

---

4. A study carried out by PricewaterhouseCoopers and referred to in the *Financial Times* noted that 'while sales of music rose 12 per cent in the first quarter of this year [2000], sales at outlets close to universities – where Napster has been popular – fell by 4 per cent' (Parkes and Grimes, 2000: 24).

investment in new bands can only be recouped through royalties received from repeated purchases by consumers of the final recording.

In July 2000, Napster was ordered by a federal judge to shut down, although the ruling was suspended pending appeal. A few months later, the battle between Napster and the RIAA took an unexpected turn when a deal was struck whereby Bertelsmann (the owner of record label BMG) withdrew its lawsuit. Bertelsmann announced that, rather than pursue its claim against Napster any further, it would instead join forces with it to develop a legal version of the service. BMG decided that it would put up $50 million to develop technology for a service based on legitimate exchanges of copyright-protected music. Bertelsmann's decision seemed to acknowledge that, irrespective of the outcome of scores of lawsuits still outstanding against Napster, the demand for online music services is not going to simply disappear. Even if the US courts succeed in shutting Napster down, dozens of imitators might well step into the gap using improved (i.e. less traceable) versions of the P2P technology originated by Shawn Fanning. So, by abandoning its lawsuit and attempting to co-operate with the pirates, BMG is hoping to find a new business model that is more in keeping with the Internet era.

The other major record companies are, however, pursing their claims with vigour. In February 2001, a US federal appeals court ruling confirmed that Napster may be held liable for copyright infringement on its system (Waldmeir et al., 2001: 1). In the same month, the European Parliament voted in favour of a new EU Copyright Directive which outlaws the distribution of copyright-protected content over the Internet (Solomons, 2001b: 12).

Nonetheless, a major lesson from Napster is that digitization and the Internet have made it more difficult, at a practical level, to exercise control over the distribution of music or any other forms of content that can be digitized. Advances in anti-piracy technologies, such as 'watermarking' or the insertion of digital codes in music tracks or other types of content, will continue to help, uphold and protect the interests of authors, artists and rights owners. But the shift to P2P networking poses risks for all sectors whose output can be stored and transmitted electronically. Since the arrival of Napster, similar sorts of technology have been devised for file-sharing of televisual content, movies and games. So, despite the protection that copyright law is supposed to provide, the question of how best to protect revenues against online piracy is one that all media content-owners have to confront.

What Napster has also shown is that within just a few months and with no marketing whatsoever, it is possible to create a highly popular Internet-based service and a globally recognized brand. Napster proved itself as a service but not as a commercial business model. The way in which P2P connects millions of PCs that had previously been isolated terminals and turns them into a network or a community of like-minded users seems to hold out great commercial promise. But, even with an enormous and growing customer base, it is not clear how a service of this sort can be turned into a profitable business.

Under the deal agreed with Bertelsmann, Napster created a membership-based service that, as of the Summer of 2001, charges users to swap and download music over the Internet. Revenue raised will be used to compensate artists, record companies and rights owners. Opinions are divided about whether and how much Internet users are prepared to pay to download music off the Internet. One commentator likened the hoped-for transition from free to paid-for downloading of music to 'starting a retail business off the back of a craze for mass shoplifting' (Solomons, 2000: 2).

The launch of Napster as a commercial service, will be followed closely by the record companies who, themselves, have begun to develop their own online distribution services (Harding, 2001a: 32). In theory, the two main possibilities are either to allow users to download songs and music on a one-off basis (but with the introduction of charges per song) or else to use a subscription model whereby members are given unlimited access to a range of music in return for, say, a monthly or annual fee. Surveys of Napster users have indicated an apparent willingness on the part of most members to pay some sort of monthly subscription, especially if this would yield a few improvements in the quality of the service (Solomons, 2001a: 10–11). Ironically then, the originator of P2P technology could also be the one who shows content providers how their businesses can adjust to exploit changing patterns of consumer demand.

nine

MEDIA ECONOMICS AND PUBLIC POLICY

S ince the earliest days of printing, the ability to communicate with
mass audiences has been subject to many forms of intervention by
state authorities. Media industries are affected not only by 'normal'
economic and industrial policy concerns (e.g. growth and efficiency) but
also by a range of special considerations that reflect the socio-political and
cultural importance of mass communications. Regulatory measures and
policy initiatives are often highly influential in determining the economic
performance of media markets and media firms. This chapter considers
what role economic theory and analysis can play in helping to address
media-related policy questions.

After studying this chapter, you should be able to:

- Identify areas where government intervention might help to improve
  the economic performance of media firms or markets
- Evaluate the use of special support measures for media content creators
- Analyse the significance of gatekeeper functions and associated
  competition concerns
- Assess the main economic arguments for and against special policies
  to restrict media ownership

FREE MARKET VERSUS INTERVENTION

The broad ideological case in favour of relying on 'free markets' to allocate
resources is based on the notion that decentralized decision-taking is

usually better than decision-making carried out by the Government. Consumers and firms are thought to be the best judges of their own interests. The price system may not always be perfect but, compared with a centrally planned economy, it is relatively effective in co-ordinating resource allocation decisions.

Even so, intervention by the Government is sometimes called for to counteract deficiencies arising from the free operation of markets. The standard economic case in favour of Government intervention in any industry is that a 'market failure' has occurred and needs to be corrected. As far as the media are concerned, the most important economic reasons why Government intervention may be required are to address market failures, to deal with the problem of externalities and to restrict the exercise of monopoly power by media firms. Of course, governments may also have cause to intervene in media markets for non-economic reasons but these are not considered here.

Many of the market failures associated with media have been discussed in earlier chapters. The most serious cases stem from the public-good characteristics of broadcast output discussed in Chapter 4. For example, based on conventional methods of market support (i.e. direct consumer payments), broadcasting might not have been supplied at all because, until very recently, it was not feasible to collect payments directly from consumers. Many broadcasting services are 'non-excludable' (which leads to 'free-rider' problems) and all exhibit the characteristic of being 'non-rivalrous'. Non-rivalrous refers to the fact that there are zero marginal costs involved in supplying the service to one additional consumer. So, to exclude some viewers leads to inefficiency and welfare losses' (Davies, 1999: 203).

Externalities are another important source of market failure in the media. These are external effects (usually costs) imposed on third parties that occur when the private or internal costs to a firm of engaging in a certain activity are out of line with its costs to society at large. The provision of some forms of media content may impose a wider cost, for example by encouraging violent or anti-social behaviour. But these costs do not have to be borne by the media supplier. The misalignment between private and social costs constitutes a market failure because it may encourage or allow too many resources to be devoted to providing media content that causes negative externalities.

In addition, other forms of media content which confer positive external affects may be under-supplied under free market circumstances. There are some types of content that are collectively desirable and that everyone benefits from (e.g. documentaries, educational and cultural output) but which audiences, on an individual basis, might not tune in to or be prepared to pay for. Various categories of broadcast output that are considered to be inherently 'good' are often treated as merit goods. A 'merit good' is one where the state takes the view that more of it should be produced than would be under conditions of market demand (e.g. health support, education).

So there are several ways in which a completely unregulated market for the supply of media might fail to allocate resources efficiently or in accordance with the best interests of society. It is up to the Government to step in with policy measures that correct these failures. As discussed earlier, two of the main policy tools used to address market failures in broadcasting are regulation and public ownership. Regulation is used to encourage privately owned broadcasters to deviate from profit-maximizing strategies where necessary in order to meet public requirements concerning the quality of their output. Broadcasters may be prohibited from supplying some types of programming that are considered damaging to society's interests and may be required to include other sorts of 'meritorious' content within their schedules. In the UK, for example, the ITC has power to impose fines on any commercial broadcaster that fails to comply with a Programme Code governing standards of content on all licensed television channels.

Another measure adopted in most countries is to organize provision of public service broadcasting through the public sector using some form of public funding. However, as discussed in Chapter 4, the use of public funds to finance state-owned broadcasting entities has become increasingly controversial in the era of multichannel competition and direct viewer payments.

Other ways in which governments can encourage the dissemination of particular sorts of media content include provision of public subsidies directed not at organizations *per se* but at encouraging production or distribution of whatever sort of content is favoured. The use of subsidies and other support measures to encourage supply and consumption of 'meritorious' content is considered in more detail below.

Finally, one of the most important concerns that arises from the free operation of markets is the accumulation of excessive market power by individual firms. As firms grow in size and gain monopoly power there is a risk that this power will be abused, with negative implications both for consumers and for rival firms. As discussed in Chapter 2, media industries will naturally gravitate towards monopoly and oligopoly market structures because of the prevalence of economies of scale. The economic characteristics of the media sector strongly encourage strategies of vertical, horizontal and diagonal growth but expansion inevitably leads to the accumulation of dominant positions by individual media firms. So, public policy interventions are required to ensure that competition is maintained and to prevent abuses of market power. Policies to counteract monopoly problems are considered in further detail below.

SUPPORT MEASURES FOR MEDIA CONTENT

The extent to which special support measures are used to encourage greater supply and consumption of media content that confers positive externalities varies from one country to the next. Across Europe, such interventions are relatively widespread and are usually aimed at creators of audiovisual content – i.e. film-makers and independent television production companies. Support measures for content creators can be divided into two broad categories. First, some policy interventions are designed to help domestic producers by restricting the volume of imports of competing non-domestic feature films and programme material. Second, an alternative policy approach is to provide subsidies to domestic producers so as to improve their competitiveness at home and in international markets.

The first approach – that of using protectionist measures – was discussed in Chapter 5. One of the main policies used to protect the European television production sector is the compulsory European programme quota set out in *Television without Frontiers*. This quota requires all broadcasters in the EU to ensure that at least 50 per cent of their transmitted output is of European origin. Measures such as quotas and tariffs will help domestic content producers by transferring demand away from imports and towards local output. The main problem with protectionism is that, by encouraging local production of goods that can be made more cost-efficiently elsewhere, it promotes what is perceived to be a misallocation of resources. Protectionism can also give rise to retaliatory measures and the risk of a tit-for-tat trade war which would leave everyone worse off.

The need to avoid waste and trade disputes is an important policy consideration in every country. But, at the same time, many countries regard cultural industries as a 'special case' and are highly concerned to preserve the positive externalities associated with the availability of domestically made audiovisual content. So, as well as subscribing to interventions that restrict audiovisual imports, many European countries also provide direct subsidies to local film-makers and television producers. The opportunity cost to society of sustaining these support measures is considerable, although subsidies for media production appear modest when compared with those allocated to sectors such as agriculture and manufacturing in recent years.

Special subsidies and taxes are effective tools for correcting any divergences that occur between private and social costs or benefits. Subsidies can be used to promote more of an activity that confers positive benefits on a wider community or on society at large while taxes help to deter activities that are costly to society. For example, a tax per unit of pollution is an effective way of encouraging firms to internalize what would otherwise be purely an externality – the cost to others of its pollution. Likewise, the provision of grants for production of locally made films in indigenous languages enables production firms to enter into their own internal calculations of costs and benefits whatever third-party gains (to local audiences) may be associated with their output. Production grants allow the positive gains to society arising from the availability of indigenously made content to be internalized by the production firm, thus correcting the failure of the market system to adequately supply such content.

European countries such as France and Germany have a long tradition of providing public subsidies and grants to indigenous producers of audiovisual content. In addition, a variety of public funding awards are available to European film-makers through schemes administered by the EU such as Eurimages and the MEDIA Plus programme. Even the UK, which generally tends to adopt a more *laissez-faire* approach towards support schemes for industry than most other EU member states, has embarked on providing large grants of public money to domestic film-makers since the late 1990s in the form of proceeds from the National Lottery.

By providing these subsidies, the aim is to try to encourage private decisions about what audiovisual content is produced to be in accordance with the wider public interest. Grants and subsidies are not only intended to encourage wider dissemination to audiences of indigenous audiovisual product but are also supposed to improve the competitiveness of domestic content-creators in home and world markets. However, some would argue that subsidies can have precisely the opposite effect. The provision of public grants for film-makers is more likely to delay and prevent the development of the skills necessary to compete in domestic and international markets than it is to improve competitiveness.

One of the main criticisms of public grants for content-creators then is that they encourage the production of films and television programming that lack commercial appeal. Subsidies for programme-makers may well help to promote wider distribution and consumption of certain kinds of 'meritorious' indigenous television content but, in so doing, they encourage local producers to depart from profit-maximizing strategies of creating content that is as popular and commercially competitive as possible.

Hoskins et al. point out that '[t]he subsidy partially insulates the producer financially from the commercial performance of the film/programme and hence lessens the motivation to be efficient' (1997: 96). If a significant proportion of production costs will be covered by a public grant then the producer has relatively little incentive to constrain the budget. In fact, if a cost-plus system of financing is favoured then producers may find it advantageous to inflate production budgets (ibid.). So, whilst special support measures can encourage higher levels of local production of audiovisual content, there is also a risk that protective interventions may prove counter-productive by, for example, contributing to a culture of dependence amongst indigenous content creators.

CONCENTRATED MEDIA OWNERSHIP

Concern about the potential for exercise of monopoly power has become an important issue for media policy-makers in recent years. Across the media industry and in related communications sectors, mergers and alliances have taken place on a massive scale and have created enormous transnational conglomerates with significant amounts of market power. Policy-makers are confronted by at least two major challenges. First, there is the question of how best to address high levels of concentrated media ownership. Are media empires a problem and, if so, how should they be tackled? As a related issue, policy-makers have been faced with the question of how to deal with monopolised control over specific access points and bottlenecks along the vertical supply chain for media.

The various advantages associated with strategies of vertical, horizontal and diagonal growth that encourage media firms to expand are discussed in Chapter 2. In theory, the main benefits that accrue to firms as they expand are to do either with increased efficiency or increased market power. Industrial economics generally attributes expansion – whether through internal growth or through mergers and takeovers – to these two key incentives associated with profit-maximizing behaviour. As far as the collective economic welfare of society is concerned, the overall impact of firms' growth strategies depends on what balance is achieved between these two possible outcomes. Efficiency gains that allow for an improved used of society's resources are beneficial to the economy as a whole. On the other hand, increased market power in the hands of individual firms poses a threat to rivals and consumers and is recognized as damaging to the public interest.

Policy-makers are sometimes confronted by the problem that proposed mergers and expansion strategies may result in *both* outcomes. For example, as a media firm enlarges, it may well be able to exploit greater economies of scale and economies of scope, thus allowing for a more productive use of resources. So consolidation appears to be warranted and desirable on the grounds of increased efficiency. Yet the greater market power associated with increased size might create new opportunities for the enlarged media firm to raise prices or otherwise abuse its dominant market position. Although enlargement may, in the first place, have been predicated on improvements in efficiency, it might well then be accompanied by the accumulation of a dominant market position which, in turn, can lead to behaviour and practices that run contrary to the public interest (Moschandreas, 1994: 483). Once a firm achieves a dominant position, the removal of competitive pressures may give rise to various inefficiencies, including excessive expenditure of resources aimed simply at maintaining dominance.

A major economic concern associated with concentrated media owner- ship is its impact on competition. Competition is generally regarded as an essential means of fostering economic efficiency and of averting abusive behaviour by dominant firms. In essence, competition – the presence of several competing suppliers – helps to ensure that firms keep their costs and prices down, which encourages a more efficient use of resources (Scherer and Ross, 1990: 20). If there are few or no rivals in a market, then suppliers can more easily get away with offering goods and services that are costly or inferior. Competitive pressures incentivize managers to improve the performance of their firm relative to rivals and this, in turn, benefits consumers and society at large. Monopolists – whether in the media or in other sectors – are usually seen as less efficient than competitive firms. Monopolists may suppress innovatory products and may, some- times, engage in 'unfair' competition.

On the other hand, a media industry in which ownership is too frag- mented is also susceptible to inefficiency. It is often argued that, because of the availability of economies of scale in the media, large firms are needed in order to ensure the most cost-effective possible use of resources. So if promoting cost-efficiency in the media industry is regarded as the dominant policy objective, then encouraging greater concentration of media ownership may be consistent with the public interest.

In short, the need to sustain competition and the desire to maximize efficiency are the two main economic policy goals affected by concen- trations of media ownership. These goals are related, in that fair and plentiful competition is seen as an essential means of sustaining efficiency. But the two objectives may pull in opposite directions. If, because of the availability of economies of scale, the optimal size of a firm in some media markets is so large as to preclude rivals, then a trade-off will occur between encouraging more competition and achieving maximum efficiency gains.

PROMOTING COMPETITION

One of the traditional concerns associated with allowing individual firms to establish dominance in particular markets is that they may charge prices that are too high and become careless about their costs (Scherer and

Ross, 1990: 19–23). Monopolists may become complacent about product quality and about the need to create new products, to the detriment of consumers. Another important worry is that dominant firms will waste too much of their resources in activities designed to maintain their market dominance. They may engage in business practices that are intended to squeeze rivals out of the market or to deter new rivals (offering products which consumers may want) from entering.

Conventional economic theory suggests that 'perfect competition' (the existence of many suppliers, in open markets, offering homogeneous products to buyers who have perfect knowledge of all available substitutes) is one route towards bringing about an efficient allocation of resources. But, in the real world, there are few if any examples of perfect competition. Very many markets in modern industrialized economies are dominated by a small number of large firms who have some degree of market power. The potential for this market power to be abused, and to result in a misallocation of resources, is the main economic rationale underlying competition policy (George et al., 1992: 314).

The media industry is prone to oligopoly and to the many forms of resource misallocation which accompany concentrated market power. In the UK, for example, very high inflation in prices charged for television advertising during the 1980s can be associated with monopolised control of commercial airtime during this period. More recently, the potential for abuse of market power wielded by gatekeeper monopolists in broadcasting – i.e. those with control over key gateways between content suppliers and viewers such as owners of predominant systems of conditional access (CAS) or electronic programme guides (EPGs) – has raised many concerns (Cowie, 1997). In addition, the price war which has affected UK national daily newspaper markets since 1993 provides an example of how dominant media suppliers may use their strength and resources to reinforce and extend positions of market dominance.

The standard provisions of national and European competition law apply to all sectors of industry including media (although public service broadcasters are often exempt). Competition policy has traditionally worked on the assumption that the efficiency of markets depends directly on their competitive structure and, especially, on the extent of seller concentration. So competition policy may sometimes involve 'structural' interventions – i.e. attempts to bring about market structures which are less concentrated – on the assumption that this will ensure good behaviour by competing firms and promote improved industrial performance (Moschandreas, 1994: 482).

Upper restrictions on levels of media ownership represent a means of structural intervention through which competition amongst media can be promoted and seller concentration can be avoided. Special restrictions on media ownership are a common feature in most European countries and elsewhere, but they usually owe their existence to concerns about pluralism and not competition. Media ownership restrictions are generally intended to protect political and cultural pluralism which, as a policy objective, is quite different from promoting competition. Nonetheless, ownership limits intended to preserve pluralism may also serve to prevent the development and subsequent possible abuses of excessive market power by dominant media firms.

The use of ownership rules to alter the structure of a market represents what some economists would consider to be a fairly extreme form of intervention. In recent years, the emphasis of competition policy has shifted away from such structural interventions towards alternative 'behavioural' measures which regulate the conduct of dominant firms in such a way as to ensure that market power is not abused. For example, the 1998 Competition Act has brought the UK approach more into line with that of the European Union, whereby the focus is on remedies to anti-competitive behaviour rather than on corporate structures (Feintuck, 1999: 91).

The change in emphasis from structural to behavioural regulation reflects important theoretical developments in the area of industrial organization over recent decades. It is now widely recognized that what matters for efficiency is not necessarily the number of rival suppliers that exist in a market *per se* but whether competitive pressure from incumbent or even potential market entrants is sufficient to induce firms to operate efficiently and to deter anti-competitive behaviour (Moschandreas, 1994: 484).

So, when interventions are called for to promote competition, ownership restrictions offer one possibility and regulation aimed at encouraging monopolistic firms into behaviour consistent with the public interest offers another. The latter approach holds out advantages in circumstances where monopolistic ownership is considered inevitable, for example in the case of 'natural' monopoly. 'A natural monopoly arises when technology is such that economies of scale exist which are exhausted at a scale of operation which is so large in relation to the market that only one firm can operate efficiently' (ibid.: 485). Where there is only room in the market for one supplier, or just a few suppliers (a natural oligopoly), this implies that increased competition would only result in higher costs and less efficiency.

Many sub-sectors of the media have some natural monopoly or natural oligopoly characteristics. The prevalence of both economies of scale and scope means that joint production – i.e. production within one firm – of a set of media outputs may well be demonstrably cheaper than their production by a multitude of separate firms. This situation presents a dilemma for policy-making. Whereas competition is generally seen as an essential stimulus to efficiency, the counter-argument may be mounted that ownership ceilings which promote competition result in an economic welfare loss by stopping media firms from realizing all available economies of scale and scope.

However, even when securing diversity of ownership involves sacrificing some potential efficiency gains, the advantages of having more than one supplier are often considered to take precedence. In the UK, the general approach towards regulation of so-called natural monopolies such as gas, electricity and telephony has changed markedly since the 1980s (George et al., 1992: 340). The postwar policy of exclusive public ownership of such activities has been reversed via a programme of privatization, regulation and efforts to promote competition. This new approach to 'the natural monopoly problem' highlights the perceived importance of introducing competitive pressures into industries that are prone to monopoly wherever this is feasible and whether or not it involves the loss of some potential efficiency gains (ibid.: 361).

MONOPOLIES AND TECHNOLOGICAL CHANGE

One of the most difficult challenges for media policy-makers in recent years has been that of how to deal with monopolies during periods of rapid technological change. The growth of the Internet and of new media has been the catalyst for a great many mergers and alliances since the late 1990s. Many large scale deals – for example the AOL/Time Warner merger or the acquisition of Endemol by Telefonica, both in 2000 – have underlined the perceived importance of developing market power across all major stages in the vertical supply chain. This has raised concern about bottlenecks, gateway monopolies and control over access to new media. According to Hughes, 'the strategic ambition of most of these players is to create vertically integrated businesses that control the gateways across TV, phone and wireless networks, offering customers a single bill, a single brand and a single EPG' (2000: 37).

The problem with monopolised control of new phases in the supply chain for media – e.g. conditional access systems, subscriber management systems (SMSs) or electronic programme guides – is that these functions are often located centrally between new service providers and viewers and so they occupy what is potentially a very powerful position. When individual firms have exclusive control over a vital activity or piece of infrastructure that all media suppliers need in order to reach viewers or to collect charges then these firms are in a position to act as gatekeepers and to decide who may or may not be allowed market access.

This has important implications for the public interest. Gatekeepers are often vertically integrated firms not only with control of the gateway in question but also with an involvement in upstream and downstream activities. The problem is that vertically integrated gatekeepers have both the means and the incentive to favour their own services and to exclude rivals. Gateway monopolists can abuse their position either by denying access to rival service providers or by offering access on terms that are very disadvantageous to potential competitors. Like monopolists in any other situation, gatekeepers have the power to raise prices, restrict output and engage in other forms of behaviour that run contrary to the interests of consumers.

The relationship between monopoly and technological innovation is not altogether straightforward. Whereas some economists believe that monopolists tend to suppress the rate of new product innovation, others (following on from Schumpeter) take the view that 'firms need protection from competition before they will bear the risks and costs of invention' and so monopoly offers the ideal situation for innovation (Scherer and Ross, 1990: 31). Schumpeter put forward the argument that the incentive of being able to reap monopoly profits, at least in the short term, is vital in encouraging firms to create new products and, thus, in stimulating overall economic growth and technological progress.

Much of the investment in new media products and new avenues for distribution of media output has come from existing large players in the media and communications industries, such as Time Warner, Pearson, Bertelsmann, BT and Telefonica. This has resulted in some cases in the emergence of *de facto* vertical and horizontal monopoly situations. For example, in the UK, BSkyB's control over the prevalent conditional access technology for pay television and its dominant position as a supplier in the market for pay-TV programming have been subject to investigation by the competition authorities in recent years.

In discussing the problems posed by regulation of gateway monopolies, Collins and Murroni point out that 'the characteristic regulatory response of imposing structural constraints on dominant firms is often at odds with the need to allow firms find their own shape during phases of transformation' (1996: 37). The high cost of activities such as laying broadband cable infrastructures or developing conditional access systems often militates against duplication by rivals, at least in the short term. Thus, structural interventions to prevent monopolised ownership of new technologies may have the unwelcome outcome of simply choking off investment and innovation.

This implies that, in order to encourage the development of new media, monopolies may have to be tolerated, at least in the short term, and their conduct regulated in such a way as to prevent anti-competitive behaviour. For some, the best response to dynamic technological change is to regulate behaviour to ensure that monopoly power is not abused (ibid.). For example, if implemented effectively, the requirement that gateway monopolists provide third-party access (for rivals to their vital facilities) on fair and non-discriminatory terms will help to promote wider market access. Under European competition law, natural monopoly bottlenecks are usually dealt with in this way under what is known as the 'essential facilities doctrine' which places a duty on monopolists to facilitate market access for rivals on fair and equal terms (Cowie, 1997).

The close interdependence of access to media content and access to distribution infrastructures has led to numerous calls for strengthened policies to tackle vertical cross-ownership. Oliver has suggested that the monopolised control of content (e.g. sports rights, movies, etc.) needed to encourage consumer take-up of new distribution systems is 'creating bottlenecks and allowing system owners to control and restrict consumer choice' (2000: 64). Likewise, Shooshan and Cave express concern that 'there is a real risk [that] viewpoint diversity will be diminished if firms with market power in distribution are allowed to extend their dominance into content/software' (2000: 12). Some favour restrictions on cross-ownership of distribution activities and those that confer gatekeeping powers. Others are concerned about the need to avoid stifling innovation by introducing too much regulation. Most, however, emphasize the need for regulators to enforce open standards and procedures that allow interconnection and interoperability between rival technologies and that safeguard access points to the media for suppliers that are independent and unaffiliated.

Regulation of technical standards (to ensure open access) and close supervision of the behaviour of dominant players are important means of avoiding problems that arise from bottlenecks and gateway monopolies. They cannot, however, guarantee that all inefficiencies associated with market dominance will be eliminated. The exercise of dominance across the supply chain for media does not simply imply the possibility of unfair pricing, vertical restraints and other restrictive practices which run contrary to public welfare. It may also involve an excessive expenditure of resources in order to gain strategic advantages over existing or potential competitors. A range of other inefficiencies, sometimes referred to as 'X-inefficiencies', may set in because of the adverse effect on managerial incentives and controls caused by lack of competitive pressure.

MAXIMIZING EFFICIENCY

Effective competition, involving many rather than just one or two rival suppliers, is clearly an ideal way to avoid the substantial range of economic deficiencies associated with excessive market dominance. To that end, the imposition of upper limits on media or cross-media ownership seems to offer useful safeguards for the process of competition and for the interests of media consumers. However, restrictions on media ownership also play a role in determining whether or not firms are allowed to reach their 'optimal' size and corporate configuration. Because of the economic characteristics of media discussed in earlier chapters, strategies of expansion within and across media industries *do*, in fact, quite often allow firms to make better use of the resources available for media provision. The fact that expansion gives rise to efficiency gains provides a compelling public interest case in favour of media ownership policies which encourage rather than curb such growth strategies.

Economies of scale are clearly a central feature of the economics of media. But the potential efficiency gains arising from concentrated media ownership do not necessarily end there. The realization of scale economies by enlarged media firms may arguably, in turn, facilitate higher levels of gross investment and speedier adoption of new technologies. Faster-growing media firms may attract better-quality personnel. Expansion strategies may create the opportunity for cost-reductions through elimination of overlapping or excess capacity (e.g. surplus printing or production capacity). In theory, all such efficiency gains represent a benefit not only for media firms but also for society at large.

The availability of a range of potential cost-savings and improvements in efficiency as media firms expand and diversify suggests that the design of media and cross-media ownership policies will have important economic implications. Ownership policies determine whether firms operating in the media industry are permitted to achieve the size and corporate structure most conducive to exploiting economies of scale and scope. Large and diversified media firms that can spread production costs across wider product and geographic markets will obviously benefit from a range of economies. A strong economic case can be made in favour of encouraging firms to exploit all such economies to the full so that waste can be eliminated and the resources available for media provision can be used to best effect. Indeed, the desire to cultivate strong and efficient indigenous media firms capable of competing in global markets encouraged media policy-makers in many European countries as well as in the USA to liberalize media ownership restrictions throughout the 1990s.

However, the concept of industrial efficiency is not just about minimizing costs. Efficiency implies producing output of the right quality and quantity to satisfy the needs and wants of society. Product diversity represents one aspect of quality. To the extent that diversity of media output is of greater value to society than uniformity of output, then some duplication of media production resources should be seen not as wasteful but as contributing to efficiency.

Special policies to deal with ownership of the media generally owe their existence to concerns about pluralism, not economics. Even so, economic arguments have gained steadily and substantially greater importance in debates about media ownership policy in recent years. Pluralism and diversity remain the key concerns underlying public policy in this area. Nonetheless, economic analysis can play a useful role by helping policy-makers weigh up potential efficiency losses caused by fragmented ownership against the benefits of sustaining effective levels of competition.

Advertising Association (1996) *The Advertising Statistics Yearbook 1996*, Henley-on-Thames: NTC Publications.

Advertising Association (1998) *The Advertising Statistics Yearbook 1998*, Henley-on-Thames: NTC Publications.

Advertising Association (1999) *The Advertising Statistics Yearbook 1999*, Henley-on-Thames: NTC Publications.

Advertising Association (2000) *The Advertising Statistics Yearbook 2000*, Henley-on-Thames: NTC Publications.

Albarran, A. (1996) *Media Economics: Understanding Markets, Industries and Concepts*, Ames, IA: Iowa State University Press.

Albarran, A. and Dimmick, J. (1996) 'Concentrations and economies of multiformity in the communication industries', *Journal of Media Economics*, 9 (4): 41–50.

Alexander, A., Owers, J. and Carveth, R., (eds) (1998) *Media Economics: Theory and Practice*, 2nd edn, Mahwah, NJ: Lawrence Erlbaum Associates.

Andrews, N. (2000) 'Lights, computers, action!' (FT Weekend Supplement p. 1), *Financial Times*, 20 May.

Bernhoff, J. (2000) 'What will be the catalysts for smart TV viewing in the digital world?', in *New TV Strategies*, London: Centaur Business Intelligence (July), pp. 10–11.

BFI (1999) *Film and Television Handbook 1999*, London: BFI.

BFI (2000) *Film and Television Handbook 2000*, London: BFI.

Blumler, J. and Nossiter, T. (eds) (1991) *Broadcasting Finance in Transition*, Oxford: Oxford University Press.

Booth, D. and Doyle, G. (1997) 'UK TV warms up for the biggest game yet: Pay-Per-View', *Media, Culture & Society*, 19(2): 277–84.

Bowler, J. (2000) 'DTV content exploitation. What does it entail and where do I start?', in *New TV Strategies*, London: Centaur Business Intelligence (July). p. 7.

Brown, D. (1999) *European Cable and Satellite Economics*, Special Report. London: Screen Digest.

Brown-Humes, C. (2000) 'Sweden's Metro spreads its free-sheet concept world-wide', *Financial Times*, 19 April: 35.

BSkyB (1996) *Annual Report & Accounts*, London: BSkyB.

Carter, M. (1998) 'Methodologies can bewilder', in the Advertising Industry, eight-page special report, *Financial Times*, 11 November: 6.

Carveth, R. et al. (1998) 'The economics of international media', in A. Alexander, J. Owers and R. Carveth, *Media Economics: Theory and Practice*, 2nd edn, Mahwah, NJ: Lawrence Erlbaum Associates. pp. 223–45.

Cave, M. (1989) 'An introduction to television economics', in G. Hughes and D. Vines (eds), *Deregulation and the Future of Commercial Television*, the David Hume Institute, Aberdeen University Press. pp. 9–37.

CEC (1997) *Television without Frontiers* (The Broadcasting Directive) 97/36/EC.

Chiplin, B. and Sturgess, B. (1981) *Economics of Advertising*, London: Advertising Association.

Choi, S., Stahl, D. and Whinstin, A. (1997) *The Economics of Electronic Commerce*, London: Macmillan Technical Publishing.

Clark, T. (2000) 'Hollywood comes to every home', in *Connectis* (FT Supplement), November: pp. 36–41.

Clarke, T. and Till, S. (1998) (Chair) *A Bigger Picture*, Report of the Film Policy Review Group, London: Department of Culture Media and Sport, March.

Coase, R. (1937) 'The nature of the firm', reprinted in O. Williamson and S. Winter *The Nature of the Firm: Origins, Evolution and Development*, Oxford: Oxford University Press, 1993. pp. 18–74.

Collins, R. and Murroni, C. (1996) *New Media, New Policies: Media and Communications Strategies for the Future*, Cambridge: Polity Press.

Collins, R., Garnham, N. and Locksley, G. (1988) *The Economics of Television: The UK Case*, London: Sage.

Competition Commission (2000) *Carlton Communications Plc and Granada Group Plc and United News and Media Plc: A Report on the Three Proposed Mergers*, Cm. 4781, London: the Stationery Office Ltd.

Corn-Revere, R. and Carveth, R. (1998) 'Economics and media', in A. Alexander et al. (eds), *Media Economics: Theory and Practice*, 2nd edn, Mahwah, NJ: Lawrence Erlbaum Associates. pp. 53–73.

Cowie, C. (1997) 'Competition problems in the transition to digital television', *Media, Culture & Society*, 19(4): 679–85.

Cowie, C. and Marsden, C. (1999) 'A comparative institutional analysis of communication regulation', in C. Marsden and S. Verhulst (eds), *Convergence in European Digital TV Regulation*, London: Blackstone: pp. 191–215.

Cowling, K., Cable, J., Kelly, M. and McGuiness, T. (1975) *Advertising and Economic Behaviour*, London: Macmillan.

Davies, G. (1999) (Chairman) *The Future Funding of the BBC*, Report of the Independent Review Panel, London: Department for Culture, Media and Sport.

Davies, P. (2000) 'Video-on demand: long time coming but now gearing up for delivery', *New Media Markets*, London: Informa Media Group, 20 October: 7.

Demers, D. (1999) *Global Media: Menace or Messiah?* Cresskill, NJ: Hampton Press.

Derecki, K. (2000) 'Narrateo set to raise £2m', *Screen Finance*, Informa Media Group, 13(20):1–2.

Doyle, G. (2000) 'The economics of monomedia and cross-media expansion', *Journal of Cultural Economics*, 24: 1–26.

Drinnan, J. (2000) 'Film Council's till plays down digital future', *Screen Finance*, 24 November: 3.

Duncan, W.D. (1981) *The Economics of Advertising*, London: Macmillan.

Dunnett, P. (1993) *The World Television Industry: An Economic Analysis*, London: Routledge.

Economist (2000) 'Untangling e-conomics: a survey of the new economy', 52-page special report, *The Economist*, 23 September.

Feintuck, M. (1999) *Media Regulation, Public Interest and the Law*, Edinburgh: Edinburgh University Press.

Financial Times (2001) Editorial comment: 'Internet profits', *Financial Times*, 15 January: 22.

Foremski, T. (2000) 'Digital interactive TV: key word is "personalization"' (IT Supplement p. 11), *Financial Times*, 5 July.

Gapper, J. (1998) 'America's networks take a stern look at prospects', *Financial Times*, 6 April: 22.

Gasson, C. (1996) *Media Equities: Evaluation and Trading*, Cambridge: Woodhead Publishing.

Gasson, C. (2001) 'Thriving new media shares? Which ones?' (Media Guardian pp. 50–1), *Guardian*, 5 February.

George, K., Joll, C. and Lynk, E. (1992) *Industrial Organization: Competition, Growth and Structural Change*, 4th edn, London: Routledge.

George, N. (2001) 'High price of newsprint is familiar reading for buyers', *Financial Times*, 9 January: 16.

Graham, A. and Davies, G. (1997) *Broadcasting, Society and Policy in the Multimedia Age*, Luton: John Libbey.

Graham, A. et al. (1999) *Public Purposes in Broadcasting: Funding the BBC*, Luton: University of Luton Press.

Greenslade, R. (2001) 'Forget the quality, feel the cuts' (Media Guardian pp. 4–5), *Guardian*, 19 January.

Griffiths, A. and Wall, S. (1999) *Applied Economics*, 8th edn, Harlow: FT Prentice-Hall.

Grimes, C. (2000) 'Fox sneaks up on rivals after an aggressive growing spurt', *Financial Times*, 16 August: 27.

Gutteridge, J. et al. (2000) 'We will fight for our rights' (Media Supplement pp. 2–3), *Guardian*, 4 December.

Hafstrand, H. (1995) 'Consumer magazines in transition', *Journal of Media Economics*, 8(1): 1–12.

Hall, E. (2000a) 'Bonanza and back', in the Advertising Industry, An FT Creative Business special report, *Financial Times*, 8 November: 3.

Hall, E. (2000b) 'Results Service', in The Advertising Industry, an FT Creative Business Special Report, *Financial Times*, 8 November: 5.

Hall, E. (2000c) 'The fever subsides', in the Advertising Industry, An FT Creative Business special report, *Financial Times*, 8 November: 6.

Harding, J. (2000) 'Online battle of the bands', *Financial Times*, 9 May: 27.

Harding, J. (2001a) 'Music labels go back to school', *Financial Times*, 31 January: 32.

Harding, J. (2001b) 'BSkyB signals move to profit generation', *Financial Times*, 8 February: 26.

Hart-Wilden, P. (1997) *A Practical Guide to Film Financing*, FT Management Report, London: Pearson.

Headland, J. and Relph, S. (1991) *The View from Downing Street*, UK Film Initiatives 1, London: BFI.

Heavens, A. (2000), 'Court settlement lifts MP3', *Financial Times*, 23 August: 25.

Hoskins, C., McFadyen, S. and Finn, A. (1997) *Global Television and Film: An Introduction to the Economics of the Business*, Oxford: Clarendon Press.

Hughes, J. (2000) 'The Global Marketplace: Making Sense of the Future' in J. Hughes et al. *E-Brittania: The Communications Revolution*, Luton: University of Luton Press. pp. 23–41.

Hughes, G. and Vines, D. (eds) (1989) *Deregulation and the Future of Commercial Television*, Aberdeen: The David Hume Institute, Aberdeen University Press.

Hydra Associates (1996) *Scotland on Screen: The Development of the Film and Television Industry in Scotland*, Glasgow: Scottish Enterprise.

Jeancolas, J. (1998) 'From the Blum-Byrnes agreement to the GATT affair', in G. Nowell-Smith and S. Ricci (eds) *Hollywood and Europe*, London: BFI.

Killgren, L. (2000) 'Purgatory postponed' (FT Creative Business p. 7), *Financial Times*, 31 October.

Larsen, P. (2000) 'Interactive TV: several important issues still need to be resolved' (IT Supplement p. 2), *Financial Times*, 7 June.

Laube, H. (2001) 'Revenge of the computer anarchists', *Connectis* (FT Supplement), February: 10–18.

Lewis, M. (2000) 'Box of tricks' (Media Guardian pp. 2–4), *Guardian*, 28 August.

Lewis, R. and Marris, P. (1991) *Promoting the Industry*, UK Film Initiatives 3, London: BFI.

Lipsey, R. (1989) *Positive Economics*, 7th edn, London: Weidenfeld and Nicolson.

Lipsey, R. and Chrystal, A. (1995) *Positive Economics*, 8th edn, Oxford: Oxford University Press.

Litman, B. (1998) 'The economics of television networks: new dimensions and new alliances', in A. Alexander et al. (eds), *Media Economics: Theory and Practice*, 2nd edn, Mahwah, NJ: Lawrence Erlbaum Associates. pp. 131–50.

Martin, S. (1993) *Industrial Economics: Economic Analysis and Public Policy*, 2nd edn, Englewood Cliffs, NJ: Prentice-Hall.

Martinson, J. (2001a) 'Dot.coms on welfare' (Media Guardian p. 72), *Guardian*, 15 January.

Martinson, J. (2001b) 'Prophets of doom at online news profits' (Media Guardian p. 58), *Guardian*, 29 January.

Meech, P. (1999) 'Advertising', in J. Stokes and A. Reading (eds), *The Media in Britain*, London: Macmillan Press. pp. 25–40.

Middleton, P. (Chair) (1996) *Report of the Advisory Committee on Film Finance*, London: Department of National Heritage, July.

Moschandreas, M. (1994) *Business Economics*, London: Routledge.

Noam, E. (1993) 'Media Americanization, national culture, and forces of integration', in E. Noam and J. Millonzi (eds) *The International Market in Film and Television Programs*, Norwood, NJ: Ablex pp. 41–58.

O' Connor, A. (2000a) 'Once more unto the breach' (FT Creative Business p. 4), *Financial Times*, 17 October.

O' Connor, A. (2000b) 'Time catches up with media's internet affair', *Financial Times*, 13 November: 26.

Ody, P. (2000) 'Sales via interactive TV: Still a novel experience' (IT Supplement p. 17), *Financial Times*, 6 December.

Oliver, M. (2000) 'e-britannia', in J. Hughes et al., *e-brittania, the communications revolution*, Luton: University of Luton Press. pp. 55–68.

O' Rorke, I. (2001) 'The audience is watching' (Media Guardian pp. 58–9), *Guardian*, 29 January.

Ostergaard, B. (ed.) (1992) *The Media in Western Europe*, Euromedia Research Group, London: Sage.

Owen, B. and Wildman, S. (1992) *Video Economics*, Cambridge, MA: Harvard University Press.

Parkes, C. (1999) 'Casualties of ratings war', *Financial Times*, 30 August: 19.

Parkes, C. and Grimes, C. (2000) 'Life after Napster', *Financial Times*, 26 September: 24.

Parkes, C. and Harding, J. (2000) 'Big prizes, big prices at the dream factory', *Financial Times*, 4 December: 25.

Parkin, M., Powell, M. and Matthews, K. (1997) *Economics*, 3rd edn, London: Addison-Wesley Longman.

Peacock, A. (1996) *The Political Economy of Broadcasting* (Essays in Regulation no. 7), Oxford: Regulatory Policy Institute.

Picard, R. (1989) *Media Economics: Concepts and Issues*, London: Sage.

Picard, R. (1998) 'The economics of the daily newspaper industry', in A. Alexander et al. (eds), *Media Economics: Theory and Practice*, 2nd edn, Mahwah, NJ: Lawrence Erlbaum Associates. pp. 111–30.

Pickard, J. (2000) 'Short change' (FT Creative Business Supplement pp. 6–7), *Financial Times*, 14 November.

Porter, V. (1999) 'Public service broadcasting and the new global information order', *InterMedia*, 27(4): 34–7.

PPA (2000) *Magazine Handbook 1999/2000*, London: Periodical Publishers Association.

Pratten, C. (1970) *The Economics of Television*, Broadsheet 520, London: PEP.

Reeves, I. (1998) 'What price fair competition?' *Press Gazette*, 30 October: 11.

Renaud, J. (1993) 'International trade in television programs: quota policies and consumer choice revisited', in E. Noam and J. Millonzi (eds), *The International Market in Film and Television Programs*, Norwood, NJ: Ablex pp. 151–62.

Rigby, E. (2000) 'Musical dispute proves far from tuneful' (IT Supplement p. 17), *Financial Times*, 1 November.

Rothwell, D. (2000) 'Switch on to the future of TV', *Investors Chronicle* 15 December: 27–9 (FT Business Publications).

Sanghera, S. (2000) 'Licensed to sell' (FT Creative Business Supplement pp. 12–13), *Financial Times*, 24 October.

Scherer, F. and Ross, D. (1990) *Industrial Market Structure and Economic Performance*, 3rd edn, Boston: Houghton Mifflin.

Screen Digest (2000a) 'European TV programme market buoyant', *Screen Digest*, April: 117–24.

Screen Digest (2000b) 'Film production and distribution trends', *Screen Digest*, June: 181.

Screen Digest (2000c) 'US dominates fragmented Euro film market', *Screen Digest*, June: 189.

Screen Finance (2000) 'Studio combined international and North American revenue from theatrical movies', *Screen Finance*, 13 October, Informa Media Group.

Shankar, V. (2001) 'Segmentation: making sure the customer fits' (Mastering Management p. 8), *Financial Times*, 22 January.

Sheldon, N. (2000) 'It's only an interactive game show!', *New TV Strategies*, August: 7, Centaur Business Intelligence.

Shooshan, H. and Cave, M. (2000) 'Media and telecoms regulation in converging markets', in Hughes, J. et al. (eds), *e-brittania: the communications revolution*, Luton: University of Luton Press. pp. 71–84.

Smith, A. (1998) 'Displaying a stronger hand', in the Advertising Industry, eight-page special report, *Financial Times*, 11 November: 1.

Snoddy, R. (1993) *The Good, the Bad and the Unacceptable*, London: Faber and Faber.

Snoddy, R. (1996) 'The renaissance that fizzled out', *Financial Times*, 25 January: 23.

Solomons, M. (2000) 'Dancing in the dark' (Creative Business Supplement p. 2), *Financial Times*, 17 October.

Solomons, M. (2001a) 'Swap shop' (Creative Business Supplement p. 11), *Financial Times*, 30 January.

Solomons, M. (2001b) 'End of the free-for-all' (Creative Business Supplement pp. 12–13), *Financial Times*, 20 February.

Sparks, C. (1999) 'The press', in J. Stokes and A. Reading (eds), *Media in Britain*, London: Macmillan Press. pp. 41–60.

Styles, P. et al. (1996) *Public Policy Issues Arising from Telecommunications and Audiovisual Convergence*, Report for the European Commission, London: KPMG.

Teather, D. (2001) 'The last mile is longest' (Media Guardian p. 52), *Guardian*, 5 February.

Tomkins, R. (1999a) 'Commercial breakdown', *Financial Times*, 5 August: 19.

Tomkins, R. (1999b) 'Handy weapon for the couch potato', *Financial Times*, 5 August: 19.

Tomkins, R. (2000) 'Advertising takes off', *Financial Times*, 21 July: 20.

Vickers, A. (2000) 'Showing at a screen near you' (Media Guardian pp. 54–5), *Guardian*, 30 October.

Waldmeir, P. et al. (2001) 'Court ruling may shut Napster', *Financial Times*, 13 February: 1.

Wedell, G. and Luyken, G. (1986) *Media in Competition*, Hamburg: European Institute for the Media.

Weymouth, T. and Lamizet, B. (1996) *Markets and Myths*, London: Longman.

White, C. (2000) 'Character building', *The Business*, 25 November: 16–22 (FT weekend magazine).

Wirth, M. and Bloch, H. (1995) 'Industrial organization theory and media industry analysis', *Journal of Media Economics*, 8(2): 15–26.

Wood, D. (1998) 'Off the shelf television', *Broadcast*, 14 August: 14.

Woodward, J. (1998) 'Our time has come', *Broadcast*, 30 January: 18–19.

Zenith Media (2001) *UK Media Yearbook 2001*, London: Zenith Media.